PRICELESS

A Teen Girl's Guide to Uncovering the
Beauty, Boldness and Brilliance Within

By

NICOLE STEELE

PRICELESS - A Teen Girl's Guide to Uncovering the Beauty, Boldness and Brilliance Within.

ISBN 978-0-9828527-0-5

Printed in the United States of America

Gem Makers
Publishing

Gem Makers Publishing
P.O. Box 461
Grayson, GA 30017

Printed in the United States of America
First Edition 2012
ISBN: 978-0-9828527-0-5

ACKNOWLEDGEMENTS
This book is lovingly dedicated to the following:

To God for EVERYTHING!!! Thank You for blessing me, keeping me, equipping me and entrusting me to do Your work. I know that without You I could do nothing and would be nothing.

To my incredible husband, Rick, thank you for being my rock and constant support and for allowing me the freedom to fulfill my dreams and purpose in life. To my two beautiful daughters, Jadyn and Victoria, I love you and thank God for blessing me with both of you. You bring me joy beyond measure. I pray that the wisdom within this book will serve as a guide all the days of your life.

Thank you to my father for your love and support. And to my wonderful mother who has served as my "real model" and an incredible example of a woman of true beauty, boldness and brilliance. Thank you for your prayers, wisdom, sacrifice and never-ending support throughout my entire life.

To all my "sistas", thank you for your prayers, encouragement and unending support over the years. And an extra special thank you to my sister, FeLicia, for affording me my weekly writing retreats. Thank you to my wonderful nieces, who I have had the joy of seeing transform into beautiful young women of God. Keep your standards high and continue to make good choices.

Thanks to Pat Hale, Bill Watt, Ann Hawkins, the Coronado family and countless others who mentored me, prayed for me and believed in me, even when I didn't believe in myself.

Last but not least, thank you to my extended family, friends, spiritual leaders, my Diamond In The Rough family, volunteers, parents, partners, supporters and the thousands of GEMS who have crossed my path over the years. Thank you for blessing my life and I pray I have been a blessing to yours.

TABLE OF CONTENTS

PRICELESS

A Teen Girl's Guide to Uncovering the
Beauty, Boldness and Brilliance Within

By

NICOLE STEELE

Chapter 1
DIAMOND IN THE ROUGH

During my lifetime, I have come in contact with thousands of girls, but none have impacted my life more than one in particular. She was the first girl who ever let me into her world and she is the inspiration for me committing my life to helping girls like her.

I remember her vividly, as if I had met her yesterday. She was your typical pre-teen girl, or so it seemed. She came from a good home and like so many in her community, she was being raised by a single mom.

Physically, she was kind of cute and no one could convince her otherwise. I recall her standing out in the crowd, in part due to her thin frame, awkward shape and extremely long legs. I remember her smile, and being almost blinded by the braces that covered her crooked teeth and the chicken pox marks that left scars across her face.

She was popular (whatever that means), super silly, boy-crazy and had lots of friends (or so-called "friends"). She could tell you all about the hottest fashions, sing the lyrics to the latest songs, and always kept up with the hottest teen trends. A social butterfly and, from all appearances, she seemed to have it all together. Nice clothes, a long list of friends and more "stuff" than she could keep track of.

She was extremely smart and a natural born leader with great potential, yet she spent most of her time following the crowd. She was bright and full of promise, but she allowed herself to simply blend in when it came to school. She was more concerned with being well-liked and fitting in, rather than standing out and being all she was created to be.

She had mastered the art of pretending. Pretending it was all good and everything in life was grand, but deep down inside she was silently struggling.

She was self-conscious about her body and spent time obsessed with the things she didn't have, instead of focusing on all the things she did have. She was desperately looking to others to validate her, and what they thought and said determined her worth and value. She put more time and attention into pleasing other people than on loving herself. The saddest part is that she always came up short.

Like many of the other girls her age, she went out of her way to make friends and was even voted most friendly in school. But what no one knew is that when she looked at herself in the mirror, she didn't like the reflection staring back at her.

I don't ever recall her actually saying she didn't like herself, but she might as well have. You see, her actions and attitude spoke much louder than her unspoken words.

Despite all her games and her ability to trick others, she couldn't fool me. I could see right through the many masks she had learned to wear so well. I knew in reality that she was insecure, unsure of herself and suffered tremendously from low self-esteem.

The truth was that she had no clue of who she really was. If she had, she wouldn't have associated with some of the people she did and she definitely wouldn't have made as many crazy and foolish choices in her young life.

I now realize what was really going on. That dear sweet girl really had a hole in her heart that started when her parents separated and it grew, and grew from there. Unknowingly, she was trying to fill that growing hole with any and everything she could to make herself feel better. The sad part is that nothing she tried worked. Instead, it led her on a downward spiral of choices and experiences she would live to regret.

She was an impressionable little girl who was trying to grow up too fast instead of enjoying life and all it had to offer. She had no real understanding of her true value and potential. I often wonder how her life would have been different, if only she had known that she was a Priceless GEM.

It was heartbreaking to see her on the fast track to self-destruction. As a teenager, she and her Mom began bumping heads and her relationship with her Dad fell apart, leaving her desperate for attention, affirmation and affection. She was really a good girl at heart and she desperately wanted to make the best choices; but the truth was her insecurities, low self-esteem and lack of self-worth only led to poor choices, unhealthy relationships, a broken heart and wasted time.

Through it all, what she was actually searching for was significance. Deep inside she didn't want to be just another girl, but how could she reach the place of contentment she so desperately longed for?

She was a "Diamond In The Rough". She was unique in design, full of potential, with value beyond measure, but she was rough around the edges, and in need of polishing. Her thoughts about herself and her future were cloudy and she wanted so desperately to blend in with the crowd. However, it never worked because she wasn't meant to be ordinary...she was created to be EXTRAORDINARY!!!

Although she couldn't see it for herself, those around her saw greatness. Her Mom, her mentors, a handful of teachers and a couple of "true" friends recognized what was on the inside and refused to allow it to go unnoticed. They could see her value and potential deep within and began working with her to bring it out. They were holding her to a higher standard than she had been holding herself to.

Over the years, with much polishing, prayers and persistence, the young impressionable teenager began her transformation from a hard, cloudy, rough diamond, into a bright, beautiful GEM. To see her today, it might be hard to believe that she is the same person.

Witnessing her transformation is the inspiration behind this book, and the fuel behind my personal commitment to help girls, just like her, all over the world. It is my heartfelt desire to help them uncover the GEM within and to find that special place where they too can begin to see their own true beauty, strength, and value, and begin to live up to their full potential.

Been There... Done That

I know first-hand the pain, emptiness and hopelessness of one who is lost, has no direction, no clear understanding of who they are and no clue of where they are going. But I also know the power, joy and strength that can only come from clearly understanding who you are and whose you are. You see, I was that girl. Yes, the "Diamond In The Rough" you read about was ME! While I've come a long way, I still have quite a ways to go.

It's my hope that as you read this book, you will gain insight and inspiration from the pages, and from my trials and struggles of insecurities. Hopefully as a result you will gain strength, encouragement and a heartfelt desire to shine brighter than ever before.

In my opinion, it's always better to learn the hard, painful lessons of life through someone else's trials and struggles, than to experience the pitfalls and setbacks first-hand. It saves so much time, heartache and pain and makes the road of life much smoother and more enjoyable.

This book was written to remind us all that our value is not determined by the way we look or the clothes we wear. It's not based on the family we were born into, the house we live in or the amount of money our parents have (or don't have). It's not based on our GPA or the people we hang out with. Our value is determined by the one who created us and who loves us dearly. I'm not referring to our parents (although they had a little something to do with creating us); but I am talking about God, the One who created you and me before the beginning of time.

Nothing happens by mistake. The fact that you are even reading this book is not by chance but by design. If you and your friends can get a clear understanding, or be reminded of just how incredible you are, there is nothing in life you won't be able to achieve. I pray that through the pages of this book, you will be introduced to the true you...the one beneath the surface. I hope you begin to view yourself in a new light and absolutely fall in love with who you see. Have

fun on the journey and get ready for greatness. It's going to be a blast!

PRICELESS PRINCIPLE - #1

Remember, you are unique in design, full of potential, with value beyond measure.

PRICELESS POINTERS
(ON BEING A GEM)

- We are all "Diamonds In The Rough", and in the right hands, with patience, polishing and persistence, we can be transformed into the bright, beautiful, brilliant GEMS we were created to be.

- Don't allow your past to dictate your future. It doesn't matter where you come from or what you've done. We all have an opportunity to start fresh and to do better once we know better.

- You are a valuable treasure and when you recognize that, others will begin to see it too.

- Remember your value is not determined by your looks, your clothes, your family, your house, or your friends. Your value was pre-determined by God.

- What you think about yourself is much more important than what others think about you.

- Choose to enjoy your life and do your very best with what you have.

Chapter 2
A PRICELESS GEM
(VALUE & SELF-WORTH)

Girls of all ages love diamonds, from the little princesses in the Disney animated cartoons to the real princesses of high society. There is just something about the sparkle and shimmer of a diamond that simply makes a girl feel good.

They've been called many things...beautiful, brilliant, and breathtaking. Whether mounted in an expensive wedding ring or draped on the necks of the Superstars walking the Red Carpet, the fact remains that diamonds are one of the most sought after gems in the world. But, beyond beauty and beyond strength, there is a word that drives home the true essence of a diamond and that word is PRICELESS. You may have heard it before but let's take a look at what the word really means.

PRICELESS
Price-less\ 'praɪslɪs —adjective

Definition: Having a value beyond any price; invaluable; precious.

Synonyms: beyond price, cherished, dear, incalculable, incomparable, inestimable, invaluable, out-of-sight, prized, rare, treasured, valuable, valued, without price.

Did you catch all that? That's pretty deep, huh? That means there is no dollar amount you can place on it. No value high enough to compare. That is pretty awesome, wouldn't you say?

And while you might be thinking of how that definition summarizes and captures the qualities of a diamond, I want you to stop and realize that the word Priceless also describes you and me. That's right! I said, the word Priceless also describes YOU and me.

Every word in that definition and the synonyms describe each of us to our core. Just like diamonds, we have value beyond any measure. Would you agree? Each one of us is a Priceless GEM, but the question is do we really believe it? And if we say we believe it, do our actions and words line up with our thoughts? In other words, do we carry ourselves as Priceless GEMS? Are we set apart or do we try hard to blend in with everything and everyone around us?

Do you believe that you are precious and rare, with a value beyond any price imaginable or does that feel so far from what you believe? The way you carry yourself, the way you speak, the people you hang around, and the way you allow others to treat you often speaks volumes about what you REALLY think about yourself.

The Million Dollar Question

Over the years, I have asked countless groups of girls how many of them would be willing to give a total stranger or someone they barely knew $1,000,000. As you probably guessed, I haven't found one girl who thought that was a good idea. It's always funny to see the eyes rolling and necks turning as girls speak with passion and conviction of how valuable money is and how there is no way they would give it away so carelessly to just anyone.

While I totally agree, I find it interesting that girls from coast to coast are willing to give a gift more valuable than $1,000,000. Many of them freely give themselves away physically and emotionally every day, never thinking about just how much more valuable they are than any amount of money.

I've learned, both personally and through observation, that when we don't know our value it becomes very easy to sell ourselves short. Some of us sell ourselves short by giving our time to things that are not worthy of our attention, like senseless gossip, mindless television, texting, tweeting, or just plain foolishness. Others of us may sell ourselves short by giving away our kisses, our bodies, our hearts, or even our souls to people who are not deserving of a gift so precious and valuable.

True Value

Many girls mistakenly place their value and worth in superficial things like popularity, their looks, their weight or how much money or material possessions they have. The problem with this is that each one of those things can change in a heartbeat. Just think about it. What's "popular" may change like the weather. If you don't believe me, all you have to do is pick up any tabloid magazine and you will see, yesterday's "somebody", is today's "nobody". The very people on the front pages of the tabloid or gossip magazines are often times the very same people once held in high esteem just a short time ago. Putting our value in popularity, trends and superficial things that are based on what others think will never work. It will always leave us empty and unfulfilled… always looking for someone else's approval and something or someone to fill that hole.

Some girls place their value in their looks or in the size and shape of their body parts. But when it comes to looks and weight, those things are always changing too (especially as you grow up and get older). If you don't believe me, just ask your Grandparents. Many of them used to have knock-out bodies and six pack abs, but you wouldn't know it by looking at them today.

As time goes on, you may gain weight or curves in certain places, or your skin may begin to change while your body goes through puberty. Oily skin, dry skin, pimples and more, are all part of growing up. The good news is that it won't last forever. The bottom line is that we should not rely on our looks to determine our worth, value or importance.

Lastly, when it comes to money and material things, we all know that no matter how much money a person has or how hard they work, it could all be lost in a heartbeat. On top of that, chances are you don't have any money anyway. While your parents may have money, unless you have a J.O.B. and are paying bills in your house, you can't lay claim to the cash. Sorry about that, but let's keep it real!

If you have found yourself basing your value on these things or giving yourself away freely, the great news is that you can shift your way of thinking and change directions, starting today. Yes, I said today! Just imagine what your life would be like if you begin to think and live like the Priceless GEM you were created to be. Would your life be different? Would it be brighter or have more meaning? Would some of the things you do, people you hang around, or the habits you have change?

In order to begin living like a Priceless GEM, you first have to have a clear understanding of the qualities and characteristics of a Priceless GEM. To make it easier to remember, I have broken it down into a simple acronym made of words that describe you.

Qualities of a Priceless GEM

 Precious - Highly esteemed or treasured.

 Radiant - Vividly bright, shining & glowing.

 Independent - Stands alone, not dependent on others.

 Classy - High quality, elegant, graceful, and dignified.

 Extraordinary - Going beyond what is normal.

 Loved - Admired, adored, treasured or cherished.

 Excellent - Very good, first class, remarkable.

 Strong - Sturdy and not easily damaged or broken.

 Significant - Important, meaningful and having purpose.

Now when you look at the qualities of a Priceless GEM, do you feel those words describe you or do you feel deep inside like you fall a little short? If you do, it's okay. I think if most people are honest, there may be an area or two where we all could grow, but regardless of how we may feel, each one of the words listed describes us the way God sees us. All we have to do is begin to line up our thoughts of ourselves with the facts.

You are one of God's greatest creations. Perhaps others around you have overlooked your brilliance and may have taken you for granted, or maybe you have even taken yourself for granted not realizing that you are special and set apart. Whatever the case, it's never too late to change your view of yourself. You can get the vision of yourself in focus today and begin to speak, walk and behave in a manner like never before. I know you've got what it takes, the question is are you up for the challenge?

PRICELESS PRINCIPLE - #2

You are a Priceless GEM whose value and potential is beyond measure.

PRICELESS POINTERS
(ON VALUE & SELF-WORTH)

❖ Post the definition of Priceless on your wall or memorize it in your heart, and remind yourself of it daily.

❖ Get in touch with who you are and make notes of what makes you special and sets you apart.

❖ Always remember that you are in a class of your own.

❖ Make it a practice to see yourself as God created you to be.

❖ Regardless of what you wear or how you look, always remember that you are fabulous, so let the world see you shine.

❖ Don't try to keep up with everyone else in the group or try to fit in with the crowd. Instead remember, you were not created to blend in, you were designed to STAND OUT.

Chapter 3
A RARE AND PRECIOUS GEM
(SELF-DISCOVERY)

Real diamonds are one of the rarest and most sought after gems in the world. Although there are many beautiful gems on earth, most people would agree that none quite compare to a diamond. Sapphires, rubies and pearls are lovely but there is just something about a diamond that sets it in a class of its own.

Well guess what? Just like a diamond, you too are in a class of your own. Have you ever stopped to think about that? Although there are over one billion girls in the world, none compare to you. Isn't that awesome? You have unique qualities, features and abilities like no other. From your eyes, to your smile, to each strand of hair on your head, everything about you is special and unlike any one else on earth.

I find it baffling when I see girls who are distinctively different and set apart spend so much time and energy working hard to look, dress and be exactly like someone else.

Although there are billions of girls in the world, none compare to you.

They spend so much time trying to measure up as a carbon copy of someone else that they fail to realize that they are a designer original.

Acres of Diamonds

It actually reminds me of a true story often referred to as "Acres of Diamonds". The story is of an African farmer who had become unhappy with his life and with what he had.

He heard that diamonds were being discovered in abundance and the idea of finding millions of dollars worth of diamonds got him so excited that he sold his farm and headed out in search of the priceless treasures.

He followed others in search of riches, wandering all over the African continent. The years slipped by as he searched for the diamonds and wealth, but it was never found. Eventually he went completely broke and in despair he threw himself into a river and drowned.

Meanwhile, the new owner of his farm picked up an unusual looking rock about the size of a country egg and put it on his mantle. One day a visitor stopped by, saw it and told the new owner of the farm that the funny looking rock on his mantle was just about the biggest diamond that had ever been found. The owner of the property told him, "The whole farm is covered with them – I've been kicking them out from under my mule."

That little farm turned out to be what is now the Kimberly Diamond Mine, which is currently the largest and the richest diamond mine the world has ever known. The original farmer had been literally standing on "Acres of Diamonds" until he sold his farm in pursuit of the very thing that he already had.

Well, the moral of the story is clear. Everything the first farmer was in search of was literally under his feet. If only he had taken the time to open his eyes and to dig a little deeper beneath the surface. Likewise, often the very thing we are seeking, lies within.

It's funny to think that sometimes the thing we are looking for is hidden in plain sight. We simply have to open our eyes, ask the right questions and use the proper tools to uncover the treasure within. The beauty, the boldness and strength we so often search for is within each of us. Each of us is standing in the middle of our own "Acres of Diamonds".

Simply Fabulous

Whether trying to live up to the images on television and in the media, or being influenced by others at school or in our community, it is important to understand that when it comes to being like someone else, no matter how hard you try, you can imitate but never duplicate. So why bother? The reality is that you can never ever be someone else, but you can focus your time and attention on being the best, most fabulous, YOU the world has ever seen.

There is always going to be someone who will be smarter, prettier, wealthier, more popular or more talented than you, but you can't let that stop you from celebrating who you are. You've got to take your eyes off other people and spend time embracing who you are and what you have to offer the world.

Do you know who you are? Do you know the greatness and brilliance that lies within you? Do you have a clue about your value and potential? Could everything that you've been looking for really be on the inside of you?

Maybe those questions have never crossed your mind, but there is no better time than the present to begin answering them for yourself.

The first step in this wonderful process of self-discovery is to recognize that YOU are precious and to understand that everything you need, you already have. You may just need to dig deep to tap into it or maybe you simply need to polish what you've got. It may take a little work and a little time but you are well worth it.

PRICELESS PRINCIPLE - #3

Although there are billions of girls in the world, none compare to you. You are precious and set apart.

PRICELESS POINTERS
(ON SELF-DISCOVERY)

- Begin to spend quality time with yourself on a regular basis.

- Make a commitment to really look at yourself at least once a day in the mirror and say to yourself aloud, "I am precious, I am powerful, I am priceless". It may feel a little weird at first, but do it anyway. It will get easier the longer you do it.

- Focus your time and attention on being the best, most fabulous, YOU the world has ever seen.

- The beauty, the boldness and strength we so often search for is within each of us.

- When it comes to being like someone else, no matter how hard you try, you can imitate but never duplicate.

- Take your eyes off other people and spend time embracing who you are and what you have to offer the world.

- No one can make you feel inferior without your consent
  – *Eleanor Roosevelt*

Chapter 4
UNIQUE BY DESIGN
(SELF-ACCEPTANCE)

Have you ever stopped to think about just how special diamonds are? Not only are they beautiful, but each one is distinctly unique and no two are exactly alike. The same is true for you and me. Every single one of us was created as a special and irreplaceable treasure.

As mentioned before, there are billions of girls on earth. Girls of all colors, shapes and sizes, but not a single soul in all the earth is just like you. From your hair, whether it's curly or straight, right on down to your twinkle toes, you are truly unique in design and distinct in all your ways. Simply put, you are a one-of-a-kind masterpiece.

Being a Priceless GEM doesn't mean that you are perfect. Even the most beautiful and most expensive diamonds have flaws. Some have flaws on the surface that are very visible to the eye, and others have flaws deep within where no one can see, but that in no way affects their ability to shine with brilliance. In fact flaws in natural diamonds add to their beauty.

As GEMS, we too have flaws and blemishes and our flaws can be caused by several things. Some of us are born with what we may consider to be flaws. Flaws in our appearance, flaws in our personality, or flaws in the family

we were born into. Others of us have flaws that were formed by things we have experienced in life. Regardless of where they come from or how long we have had them, the question is what are we going to do about them?

Don't Let Your Flaws Freak You Out

We have a choice in life, to allow our flaws to freak us out or embrace them and let them work in our favor. There will be things in life that you can work hard on perfecting and other things that you won't be able to change no matter what you do.

What things in your life would you like to change if you could? Are they physical flaws that you were born with that set you apart, or do you have habits and hang-ups that you would like to change?

If a few things come to mind when thinking about that question, the first thing you have to ask yourself is, "What is my motivation in wanting to change these things?" Do you want to change those things because other people want you to? Do you want to change because people make fun of you? Do you want to change so you can be liked by others or fit in with a particular group, or do you genuinely want to change things for yourself? The second thing you need to ask yourself is, "Can the things I want to change actually be changed?"

If we determine that we want to change things in order to be accepted by others, the best thing we can do is to stop while we are ahead. As long as we live there will be critics.

People will have constructive criticism that can help us be better and shine brighter, but there will likely be more people who are just down-right haters and you will never meet their approval, no matter what you do. In most cases these people are critical of others because in reality they are really unhappy with themselves.

Thinking back, I went through a phase when I was young, when I didn't enjoy being tall. For me it was always awkward towering over my classmates, especially most of the boys my age. But what I eventually realized was that there was absolutely nothing I could do about my height. I came from a family of tall people and that was just a fact of life.

I allowed a few taunts and teases from a handful of goofballs in my class to get me stressed over nothing. It's crazy how I let someone else's insecurities become my issue. Because several of them were short, it was easier for them to make fun of me, but in reality millions of women and girls buy high heels everyday to be tall and to get a view of the world from my perspective.

By changing my way of thinking I began to stress less over my height, and instead began to embrace it. Before I knew it I began to celebrate and appreciate being tall and now, I actually love it.

What I learned from that experience is that we need to make it a point to rock what we've got. Whether we have short legs or long, thick lips or thin, thick hair or thin, we need to learn to strut our stuff with confidence and be comfortable in the skin that we are in.

We should work to change the things we can and learn to be content with the things we cannot change. When we understand this simple Priceless Principle it makes the journey of life much more enjoyable.

Stop Competing and Comparing

When it comes to diamonds there are so many shapes, sizes and colors to choose from that for the average buyer, making a selection can sometimes be difficult, overwhelming and down-right confusing. Well just as one can get weighed down with comparing real diamonds, we can also get distracted and off course by competing and comparing ourselves with others.

Competition is part of human nature and can be useful in helping us sharpen our skills and become better. However, it can turn into a real problem when we become obsessed in comparing ourselves to others. I once heard a Pastor named Ed Young say, "It's unfair to compare", and if you think about it, he is right. It is unfair to the person you are comparing yourself to, who in most cases doesn't even know they are being judged or rated. But in addition to that, it is also unfair to you.

More times than not, when we compare ourselves to others, we end up magnifying our own flaws which are often blown out of proportion and made bigger than life. On top of that, when we compare ourselves to others it's a slap in the face to God who created us. It's like us saying that He made a mistake when He created us, which is far from the truth.

Many girls today have so much value and potential, but they don't realize it. They often base their value on how they size up to other girls. What other girls look like, who they hang out with, what they are wearing, what they think or what they say. Have you ever struggled with comparing yourself to other girls? If you are honest, the answer is probably yes, and what that simply means is that you are not alone.

It's funny how we can strive so hard trying to be like someone else instead of celebrating who we are and what we have to offer the world. I see it in so many instances. So often, girls with curly hair want straight hair, and girls with straight hair are doing everything possible to make it curly and full. Those with red hair wish they were blond, while those with light hair add color to make theirs darker. Often times, short people wear heels to make themselves taller. While on the other hand, many tall people shrug their shoulders downward instead of standing tall, or they tend to wear flat shoes so they don't stand out like giants.

A Life Long Lesson

We could go on for days listing things that girls obsess over, from wishing they could change their skin tone, to changing their breast or butt size. If I had a penny for every minute the average teenage girl spends trying to look like, dress like and act like someone else, I would be a multi-millionaire.

Often while we are trying to be like someone else, there is someone else trying to be just like us.

Well, here is a newsflash for everyone. We will never succeed at being someone else, no matter how hard we try. The funny thing is, often while we are trying to be like someone else, there is someone else trying to be just like us.

I wish I had known this when I was young. I spent an enormous amount of time wishing I was shorter, wishing I was more developed in certain areas, and less curvy in other areas. The insecurities I had were so many that I can't begin to count them all. Name the insecurity and chances are I faced it. I thought my life would be perfect if only I could be like the other girls around me.

I was consumed with clothes and put a lot of unnecessary pressure on my mother to buy me the latest and greatest fashion, knowing she was struggling as a single parent. Looking back, I can't believe I was so insensitive and clueless about what really mattered.

All that energy, wasted time and money was driven by my obsession to be like the others around me instead of realizing that I was complete just the way I was. What I didn't know was that although I could never ever be the best at being someone else, I could be 100% successful at being me, with my long legs, flat chest, awkward body shape and all.

God knew exactly what He was doing when He created me. From my brownish red hair that changes colors at different times of the year, to my long narrow feet, to the chicken pox scar in the middle of my face. Everything about me was

made marvelously, and guess what? Everything about you is marvelous too.

The bottom line is that if God wanted us to be clones of each other He would have made us that way. Instead He made us distinctly different because He loves variety. It shows when we look around during the springtime and see a variety of flowers in every color, scent and shape imaginable, and leaves of every color in the fall.

We can see the uniqueness of God's creation in everything from the birds in the sky to the array of colors of diamonds found beneath the earth's surface. Did you know that diamonds are created in almost every conceivable color? Yes, it is true. They also come in red, yellow, blue, black, green and my personal favorite...pink.

Just think, if He cared enough to create such variety in these things, how much more does He delight in creating each of us unique in design? Have you ever thought about what an insult it is for us to say to the very One who created us, "Hey, I'm not happy with how You made me!" It's almost like spending your precious time and hard earned money to purchase a special unique gift for a loved one, and as you await their response, they open the gift, turn to you with a frown and say, "Oh, is this it? I was hoping for something else." Can you imagine how sad and disappointed you would feel? Well it's no different when we minimize our value and worth in comparison to that of someone else. We are a gift created by God!

Don't Be Fooled

On the surface, making comparisons may seem innocent and harmless, but in actuality it is a seed that can grow and lead to a life of misery and defeat. When we compare ourselves to others, it keeps us distracted and off course. Comparison and unhealthy competition can make us prideful or pitiful. It either makes us wish we had what another person has or it leaves us feeling like we are better because of what we have.

The really sad thing is once you begin comparing yourself to others, it's hard to stop and can actually be like a lifetime prison sentence. It may begin with the simple comparison of clothes, hair and shoes but can grow into obsessive comparisons of houses, husbands, cars and kids. It can totally overtake you and become an obsession that creates dissatisfactions that steal your joy and happiness.

Instead of competing and comparing, why not let your admiration become motivation. For instance, if there is a girl who has style or who is one of the smartest students in your class, compliment her on her style or congratulate her on her achievements. Instead of comparing yourself in a manner that makes you feel less than, or may even make you a little envious, take that same energy and allow it to inspire you to be better and to shine brighter. Like the saying goes, "Don't hate. Celebrate!"

PRICELESS PRINCIPLE - #4

Work to change the things that you can and learn to be content with the things you cannot.

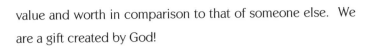

value and worth in comparison to that of someone else. We are a gift created by God!

Don't Be Fooled

On the surface, making comparisons may seem innocent and harmless, but in actuality it is a seed that can grow and lead to a life of misery and defeat. When we compare ourselves to others, it keeps us distracted and off course. Comparison and unhealthy competition can make us prideful or pitiful. It either makes us wish we had what another person has or it leaves us feeling like we are better because of what we have.

The really sad thing is once you begin comparing yourself to others, it's hard to stop and can actually be like a lifetime prison sentence. It may begin with the simple comparison of clothes, hair and shoes but can grow into obsessive comparisons of houses, husbands, cars and kids. It can totally overtake you and become an obsession that creates dissatisfactions that steal your joy and happiness.

Instead of competing and comparing, why not let your admiration become motivation. For instance, if there is a girl who has style or who is one of the smartest students in your class, compliment her on her style or congratulate her on her achievements. Instead of comparing yourself in a manner that makes you feel less than, or may even make you a little envious, take that same energy and allow it to inspire you to be better and to shine brighter. Like the saying goes, "Don't hate. Celebrate!"

PRICELESS PRINCIPLE - #4

Work to change the things that you can and learn to be content with the things you cannot.

Chapter 5
MIRROR MIRROR
(SELF-IMAGE)

Have you ever seen a funhouse mirror at the carnival, you know the type that makes everything about you look crazy? Well, sometimes it's as if the mirror in the bedrooms and bathrooms in our homes are a lot like those at the funhouse.

For some of us, when we look in the mirror, we see a million and one things that are wrong, instead of seeing the reflection of our true beauty. Every flaw, every blemish, every imperfection is magnified a hundred times over. Every pimple and every dimple seem larger than life. If we aren't careful, before we know it we find ourselves focusing on all the things that are wrong instead of on the long list of things that are right.

When was the last time you looked in the mirror? I'm not talking about just a quick glance as you walk out the door or as you quickly brush your teeth before bed (and I do hope you brush your teeth before bed). I am asking when was the last time you took a nice long look at yourself and

really admired what you saw. If it's been a while, I challenge you to stop and take a minute to do it now. I'm serious, put the book down and do it right now.

STOP!

Find the largest mirror and go look at yourself for at least three minutes from head to toe. When you are finished, pick up reading where you left off.

Okay, how was it? Was it difficult to look at yourself? Were you super critical, thinking about the long list of things you wish you could change about yourself? Well, if so, it is my hope that by the time you finish this book you will be able to look in the mirror and truly love what you see.

Moving forward, I want to challenge you to make a habit of looking at yourself in the mirror a couple of times a day. I want you to begin to speak to yourself in the mirror and remind yourself of how brilliant, bright and beautiful you are.

To remind yourself, you can write it on the mirror (unless you share your mirror with someone else). Another thing you can do is write it on an index card or piece of paper in your favorite color marker and tape it on the mirror as a reminder. While it may be challenging at first or seem a little weird, it will get easier every day. Hopefully one day it will become second nature to love and embrace the reflection staring back at you.

PRICELESS PROCLAMATION

I am Brilliant, Bright & Beautiful

Although it may be an awkward time in life with all the changes going on physically and hormonally in your body, it is important for you to realize that you are absolutely fabulous with your own unique qualities and incredible potential. You are not just an average girl, you are complete all by yourself.

You are a magnificent, matchless and marvelous creation, created in the image and likeness of God. If you don't believe me check it out for yourself in Genesis 1:27. I don't know about you, but being created in the image of the God, who created the entire universe and everything in it, must mean that we are pretty awesome.

You are set apart in a class of your own. Just like a rare diamond, you are to be protected, respected, held in high esteem and handled with care. You are a valuable treasure, so don't ever let anyone tell you otherwise.

Distinguished Beauty

Many things help to shape our definition of beauty and success, and we can be influenced by fashion magazines, videos, television, or Hollywood trends. Unfortunately, it's not only the media. There are other factors that can play a part in how we define beauty and ultimately determine how we feel about ourselves. It can often be influenced by what we have been taught by members of our family, our friends, our classmates or the culture.

When it comes to real beauty, it is much bigger than just our outer appearance which is made up in part by our looks, our clothes and the way we wear our hair. Girls and women with true beauty have something that penetrates beyond the surface and shines from within. They sparkle with personality and they have confidence in who they are and also understand whose they are.

They are strong beyond measure and possess individual charm. They brighten the places they go and they allow themselves to be molded and shaped in positive ways through their experiences. They have character and their values carry weight.

That's what you call real beauty, true beauty that surpasses the trends of today and the opinions of others. It's more than skin deep and it is the beauty that we all need to strive for.

Do you find yourself focused on your weight, keeping up with the latest fashions or maintaining your hair and nails? If your answer is yes, I'm sure you agree that it can be both time consuming and expensive.

Although it is important to take care of ourselves and to strive to be our very best, it must be kept in balance. There is absolutely nothing wrong with wanting to look your best and keeping yourself healthy by working out and eating healthy. If you find yourself doing it to please someone, to be like someone else or you become obsessed to the point where nothing else in life matters, you need to give your head a shake and snap out of it.

While there are some things that girls shop for at the mall to make them look and feel beautiful, there are many things that cannot be bought, things like kindness, honesty, fairness, and integrity. We should spend as much or more time focusing on building and shaping our inward beauty. True beauty is really based on what is on the inside, because what is on the inside will ultimately begin to show on the outside.

For instance, have you ever known someone who is physically attractive and maybe even well-dressed, but the minute they open their mouth your picture perfect image of them totally changes? How about the person who looks nice but whose attitude or mouth is so foul that it changes your level of respect for them?

On the other hand, have you ever met someone who marches to the beat of their own drum? Perhaps they have a style of their own or wear their hair in a way that is quite different than anyone else you know. Even though people may look at them strangely from time to time, they have a confidence or a personality that outshines them all. Despite what others think about them, it in no way affects the way they feel about themselves.

Living Life from the Inside Out

Our goal should be to live our lives from the inside out. This simply means that we should strive to be young women of confidence and great character, focusing more on building inner qualities than on the external things. We should carry ourselves in a way that doesn't say we are without fault, but does say that we are priceless with value beyond measure.

Once we realize it deep down in our hearts, then our words, our actions and our choices will begin to reflect that. While it may seem a little tough to imagine ourselves thinking and speaking differently about ourselves, it really is a fairly easy thing to begin doing. You are the only one who can begin the change and the power is in your hands. Now, the question is, what will you do with it?

PRICELESS PRINCIPLE - #5

Remember, real beauty shines from the inside out.

PRICELESS POINTERS
(ON SELF-IMAGE)

❖ Love yourself just as you are because God does.

❖ Remember, when you criticize how you look, you're actually criticizing God, and in essence saying He didn't do a good job when He created you.

❖ Make an effort to look at yourself every day and choose one thing you especially like.

❖ Define your own concept of beauty. Don't let others set the standards for you.

❖ Real beauty is more than just how you look on the outside. It's what you have going on inside.

❖ Try to live your life from the inside out.

❖ Everything you say and do communicates something about you, so be careful of the messages you send.

Chapter 6
THE GREAT TREASURE HUNT
(SELF-ESTEEM)

One of my husband's favorite television shows is The Antique Road Show. I'm not sure if you have ever seen it but, if not, you should check it out sometime. It features people from all over the country who bring odd items in to have them appraised by experts. Often times they are things that have been purchased at garage sales, found in attics or left by loved ones who have passed away. By all appearances most of the items look old, worn-out and worthless. But a real expert who has a trained eye can clearly distinguish between trash and treasure. I am always amazed to see people come in with items they thought were worthless, only to find out that they have value beyond their wildest imagination.

Perception Is Reality

It's funny how our perceived value of something can affect the way we look at it and even how we take care of it. It makes me think about many children who throw their clothes or toys around,

giving little thought to how much they cost or how hard their parents worked to provide them. They don't really see a big deal because they didn't work to pay for it with their own money. But the game totally changes when it comes to something they have saved for and purchased with their hard-earned money or allowance.

For instance, when one of my nieces was in high school and finally got a car, I was amazed at how clean and clutter-free it was each time I rode with her. You can bet your bottom dollar that you would never find candy wrappers and empty Coke cans on the floor or between the seats. She took care of that car inside and out and kept it spotless. She kept it washed and waxed and made sure she kept the gas tank full and the oil well maintained.

While I was very proud of her for being responsible, it proves my point that when someone truly understands the value of something, it affects the way they treat it. On the other hand, when a person has no clue of the value of something, they often tend to mistreat it, abuse it or neglect it.

The same is true when it comes to the way we see ourselves. If we don't value ourselves or recognize our worth, it can directly or indirectly affect the way we treat ourselves and the way we allow others to treat us.

Uncovering the True Treasure Within

Can you think of a person who, from all appearances, looks as if they had the ideal life? You might even be that person, who everyone around you admires and thinks is living the picture perfect life. Always smiling on the outside, but deep on the inside you are thinking to yourself... "There must be more to life than this".

I know what that feels like because for years that person was me. I had no clue of who I was nor did I understand my value. I remember vividly the insecurities and self-doubt I felt. Although, on the outside I may have appeared confident and self-assured, it was so far from the truth. Deep down inside I was searching desperately for significance, instead of realizing that everything I needed, I already had. I simply had to uncover it.

Buried Treasures

Every single one of us has that special treasure hidden within, but only with patience, persistence and polishing can it be brought to the surface for the entire world to see.

What's up with your treasures? Are they exposed for the world to admire, or have they been buried somewhere along the way. Whether buried underneath layers of false images, insecurity, lies, and self-doubt, or because of the careless words or actions of family members, friends or others, the good news is that you can begin to uncover your very own buried treasures today. It is as simple as making a decision to change the way you see and speak about yourself.

As you read the pages of this book, only you can decide what you will do with the Priceless Principles listed. Others around you can see your value and potential, but until you see it for yourself and begin to walk in it, it doesn't matter. When you begin to see yourself in a new light it can totally transform your life in an incredible way. I know because it changed mine. Growing up, I had no clue of my value, true potential or worth, and because of that, I depended on others to validate me. Can we say, bad idea?

I double dare you to open your mind as you read this book and begin to see yourself as the Priceless GEM you were created to be. Get rid of any negative thoughts you have ever had about yourself, whether they were planted by you or by others.

If you just happen to be the type of girl whose self-esteem is sky high and who never has negative thoughts about yourself, then this book should simply confirm what you already know.

True Identity

In a world of false images, airbrushed advertisements and reality television, it is easy for any girl to be overwhelmed as she seeks to figure out who she is and how she fits into the big world. If that sounds like you, let me share a secret with you; you are not alone. The good news is you don't have to stay there.

You don't have to have the same story as me and so many others who have spent decades wandering around lost and misguided. Instead, you have an opportunity to by-pass years of wasted time, misery and mistakes and be introduced to the real you and to begin to love who you see.

The True Virtues of a Diamond

I find it interesting that if you ask the average female from ages nine to ninety to describe a diamond, in most cases they would give a long list of words all painting the picture of something of extreme beauty and value. Yet, if you ask those same people to describe themselves, the words often chosen would be the total opposite.

Just think about it for a minute. Do girls your age typically walk around saying positive, up-lifting words about themselves or are most of the comments they make about

themselves harsh and cruel? You know the comments I am referring to. Comments like, "I'm so fat..."; "I hate my hair..."; "Ugh, look at my butt..."; "Everyone hates me...", etc. Whatever the comments, in most cases when it comes to the way girls talk about themselves, the words are often critical and in many cases, far from the truth.

We can often be our own worst critic. Yes, we all have things we would like to change or improve, but the reality is that we often have more going for us than against us. It's all about our perspective. In fact, when it comes to the qualities of a diamond, no matter who we are or what our story, we actually have more in common than we may think.

- Diamonds are Beautiful
- Diamonds are Brilliant
- Diamonds are Strong
- Diamonds are Unique
- Diamonds are Full of Value
- Diamonds are Extraordinary
- Diamonds are Multi-faceted
- Diamonds are Set Apart
- Diamonds are Timeless
- Diamonds are Loved

All of those things not only describe natural diamonds but they are words and phrases that also describe you and me. Whether we realize it or not, those are qualities that we were born with, that were placed within us before the beginning of time. The question is does your personal identity line up with that fact?

It is wonderful to fall in love with yourself and to have a clear understanding of how very special you are. I'm not talking about being arrogant and cocky. I am talking about having true confidence that can't be shaken or taken by the careless words or thoughts of others. There really is nothing quite like coming into a clear understanding of who and Whose you are.

It's as simple as lining your thoughts and personal image up with that of the One who created you. The reality is that God molded you together in excellence, with no detail left out. Every cool and quirky thing about you was created by design. Whether you see it or not, you were made perfect in His sight. He even knows the number of hairs on your head (Luke 12:7).

He knew you before your parents ever met. He hand-crafted you in excellence before the beginning of time and He appointed the very hour and day that you would make your debut here on earth. He equipped you with gifts, talents and abilities and He has also given you dreams and visions to do things, some of which may never have been done before. Despite your situation or circumstance, no matter your family or financial situation, the bottom line is God loves you and His plan for your life is good.

So, grab hold of that and highlight it in this book and hide it in your heart. Don't worry about what the magazines and the media say, or even what a "ding dong" or two have said to your face or behind your back. Instead, remember what the Creator of the universe says about you. And remember that the very same qualities that describe diamonds are the same that describe you and me.

PRICELESS PRINCIPLE - #6

Remember, the value we place within ourselves determines the way we treat ourselves and the way we allow others to treat us.

PRICELESS POINTERS
(ON SELF-ESTEEM)

⬧ Your true identity is based on how you see yourself.

⬧ It's important to know that you are a person created in the image of God and He has certain expectations for your life.

⬧ When God created you He gave you certain gifts and talents, all of which have great value.

⬧ How you live your life on the outside reflects what's in your heart.

Chapter 7
FROM ROUGH TO RADIANT
(SELF-EXAMINATION)

Have you ever visited the mall and passed a jewelry store only to be mesmerized by the dazzling diamonds in the display cases? It's no wonder they can demand the high price tags that go along with them. But have you ever given any thought to where diamonds come from or the time and energy it takes to transform them from rough to radiant?

Don't Miss It

If you have never seen a rough diamond before it is transformed, it would surely shock you. Most people wouldn't be able to recognize a rough diamond if it was staring them in the face because they are typically cloudy, unformed and easily overlooked and mistaken for any old rock. In fact, if you ever came across one, I can pretty much guarantee you would probably step over it, kick it, or totally ignore it all together.

However, a trained eye can see that same rough diamond and see beyond its current state to recognize its hidden value and potential. The fact that no one else realized it and many may have walked over it makes no difference. The fact remains that a diamond is a diamond and its value remains the same whether someone recognizes it or totally overlooks it.

Just as with real diamonds, we too have value that most could never imagine. However, if we aren't careful we can also overlook our own value or discount it tremendously. At a glance we may appear to be normal or just like any other girl in the crowd but, in actuality, just beneath the surface there is endless value and potential. The great news is that in the right hands, with the proper tools and by taking time to go through the process we, like a rough diamond, can be transformed into a bright, beautiful, brilliant GEM.

Digging Deep

Diamonds are considered rare because they are very hard to find. They are created at very high temperatures under great pressure and can only be found by digging deep beneath the earth's surface. To find them, it takes precision, care and a lot of hard work.

Don't be afraid to dig deep. It is in the deep places that the greatest treasures are found.

Finding girls who are truly confident is also rare and very hard to find. I'm talking about girls who have a confidence that goes beyond the surface and penetrates to their hearts and souls. This kind of confidence can only come from having a clear understanding of who you are, and in order to do this a girl has to be willing to dig deep. By digging deep she is able to begin to embrace the things that are unique about her and become more clear about the things that matter most.

Once you start digging you can never predict what you will find. On top of that, the deeper you dig the more you are likely to find. I don't say this to discourage or freak you out, but instead to excite you. As you begin to dig deep I hope that you will uncover things about yourself that you never would have imagined. Whether it is a passion for something new or breaking an old habit, the process of digging deep can work to your advantage and truly pay off in the end.

Patience Through the Process

Diamond miners use expensive machines to drill down in the earth in search of hidden treasures and they always end up extracting much more in the process. They have to carefully sift through all the dirt, rocks and debris in order to find the prized treasure within. In digging deep within ourselves, sometimes we can also uncover some junk we weren't intending to find.

Digging deep may seem overwhelming and leave a girl wondering just where in the world to start. If this sounds like you, don't stress. It simply starts with you making up

your mind and taking the first step. Just as with a real diamond, after you dig deep, then comes the cutting and polishing process.

This process can often be long and sometimes painful because it requires us to be honest with ourselves, and the reality is that we may not always want to do that. Some people enjoy living in La La Land and others just flat out don't want to go through the process. Some girls are okay with just living an average, dull, boring, unfulfilled life. How about you?

Preparing for Polishing

We could all use a little shaping in one area of our lives or another to help us shine brighter. Wouldn't you agree? For some of us we may need to polish our attitude. Others of us may need to make changes in the way we carry ourselves.

There are some of us who may need to polish up on the way we think or maybe the way we talk about ourselves to others. Then again there may be others of us who may need to simply change our environment and stop hanging around with people who are a negative influence. Regardless of our personal situation, going through the process can be painful at times, but it is well worth it in the end.

To begin the process you have to start by taking an honest look at yourself, and in order to do that you have to spend a little time with yourself. Yes, that may mean turning off the television, putting your cell phone down, shutting off Facebook, and placing a timeout on texting. You may be wondering, why is that necessary? Well, it's because all those things often represent noise and distractions in life. They are also filled with other people's opinions and expectations. By spending time with yourself, you are able to shut off the influences of others, and begin to understand what's important to you and why.

It requires us to remove the many masks we sometimes wear and to take a real good look at ourselves. It may also require us to take a look at those around us and to make some tough decisions about the people we call our friends, especially if their lives are heading in a different direction than ours.

What type of life do you want to live? Are you living that life now? What are your hopes and dreams for your future? What is important to you? All these questions are important

We could all use a little shaping and polishing in one area of our lives or another to help us shine brighter.

and are questions that only you can answer.

Would you say you are living your best life now? If not, what are you waiting for? Are you willing to be honest with yourself? Are you willing to make positive changes today that will benefit you for years to come?

I'm not talking about making changes because your family or friends want you to, but making changes because you want to. Your future is bright and the possibilities are endless. The question is, are you up for the task?

I have confidence that you can do it, but it's not enough for me to believe these things. You have to believe that you can do it too and that you are worth it. Frankly, I think you have what it will take and I also think that when it's all said and done, you will be stronger and shine brighter than even you could have imagined. So roll up your sleeves and get to work. Your destiny is waiting.

Girl, Watch Your Mouth

When I was young, I remember times when my grandmother would get excited and say, "Girl, you better shut your mouth". Now she didn't mean that literally, it was only a figure of speech. However, when I hear some of the things that come out of the mouths of girls today, it makes me want to both say it and mean it too.

There are many things in life that we have no power to control. For instance, we can't control the family we were born into, certain physical traits we are born with, or certain quirks in our personality. Nor will we ever be able to control the haters in life who don't like us for one ridiculous reason or another.

However, there is one thing that we have total control over and that is the words we speak. The tongue is one of the smallest organs in the human body, yet it is one of the most powerful. With our mouths, we have the power to build up or tear down. So if that is the case, why are we so careless in what we say?

It's been said that a person's words say a lot about them. If I were to listen in on your daily conversations, what would your words reveal about you? Do you engage in mindless conversation or gossip?

How do you speak about yourself? Are the words you speak about yourself uplifting and affirming or harmful and degrading? If your words aren't positive, I challenge you to begin to change them immediately. Simply taking control of your thoughts and the words you speak can literally change your life.

I'm sure you can think of someone whose words are poisonous, and like a venomous snake. When they open their mouths they leave people in their paths worse off.

You can also probably think of someone whose words are uplifting and powerful. It may be a family member, a teacher, a coach or a friend. And perhaps, when you are around them, you usually come away feeling better, stronger or happier by having been in their presence.

If your friends or family had to place you in one of those two

categories, which would it be? When you open your mouth, what's the result? Would they describe you as a person who brings negativity everywhere you go, or as a person who is a joy to be around and is an inspiration to all they come in contact with?

Think it→ Say It→ See It→ Be It

Everything in life begins first with a thought. Every bright idea, great invention or historical movement began with someone first thinking about it. On the same note, every bad and negative thing in life also starts with a thought. Where your mind goes, your actions will likely follow. I'm sure if we are honest, we can all think of a time when that was true.

For instance, have you ever felt a little under the weather and begun to complain to family and friends about how horrible you feel and how you think you are getting sick? And then before you knew it you really were sick.

How about when it comes to school? Have you ever taken a test and gone into it telling yourself and anyone who would listen, "I'm going to fail"? Then when you get the test score back you got exactly what you asked for and spoke into existence.

Well, the same principle applies when you speak positively over certain situations and begin to look at them from a positive perspective. While you still might have challenges, just having a change in attitude and in the words you speak, can make all the difference in the world.

There really is a simple way to change your behavior. You may remember in elementary school, a teacher saying, "If you don't have anything nice to say, don't say anything at all". It really is just that plain and simple.

Think before you speak, and ask yourself if what you are about to say will be powerful, purposeful or poisonous? If you think the things you are about to say about yourself, your situation or someone else are negative, kindly zip your lips.

PRICELESS PRINCIPLE - #7

Remember your thoughts become your words, your words become your actions and your actions determine your destiny

PRICELESS POINTERS
(ON SELF-EXAMINATION)

🔹 Your future is yours. Own it!

🔹 When it comes to your future, remember, what you put into it is what you will get out of it.

🔹 In order to reach your goals, first you have to have goals.

🔹 If you never attempt more than you've done, you will never get more than you've got.

🔹 Write your plan and work your plan. Create the vision you have for your life and write your goals and how you plan to achieve them.

🔹 Make an appointment with yourself once a week to track your progress on meeting your goals.

🔹 Be intentional about your words, and remember, there is power in words so be very careful about what you say about yourself and others.

Chapter 8
WE ARE JEWELS, NOT TOOLS
(SELF-RESPECT)

It's been reported that for every ton of diamonds used to make beautiful jewels, there are four more tons that are used as tools. Because diamonds are one of the hardest substances on earth and don't easily wear down or break, they are often used to manufacture many of the household items that we come in contact with everyday. These items include saws, drill-bits, computer microchips, electrical components, x-ray machines, lasers, audio speakers, and more.

Don't Be Fooled

While it is great and a necessity for real diamonds to be used as tools for multiple purposes, it is not okay for us to allow ourselves to be used by people or for purposes we weren't created for.

In a society that often exploits women and girls in everything from daily advertisements, movies, television programs, music videos and video games, it is vitally important that we don't get tricked into thinking that we are mere tools to be used by others and handled any kind of way.

The Webster's dictionary defines the word "Tool" as "one that is used or manipulated by others". Isn't that interesting? It clearly describes the situations many girls find themselves in everyday.

Just think about the commercials, billboards, magazine advertisements and movies you see, or how about the songs and lyrics in much of today's music. Everywhere we turn in our society, young women and girls are being used as tools to sell items and make money for others.

If you really think about it, you would notice that it often starts when we are young with many of the dolls, cartoon characters and pop idols. And as we grow older the products change but the tactics remain the same. You can find examples everywhere, from the automotive magazines and advertisements with beautiful half-naked models laying on the hood of the shiny new car, to the music videos where all the guys are fully dressed but all the women are wearing close to nothing as they bump, grind and drop it like it's hot. Women and girls are being used, some against their will and others by their choice. What's up with that? It's not right.

I think about how often girls are tricked into believing that their worth and value is based on how "hot" they look or how much skin they can show. They use their bodies and sex as a tool to get attention, love, affection and other things, instead of understanding how truly precious they are.

Tools vs. Jewel

When you think of the contrast between tools and jewels it's quite interesting.

Tools	Jewels
Definition: One that is used or manipulated by others	**Definition:** One who is highly esteemed and valued
Man-made	God-made
Mass produced	One- of- a- kind
Common, ordinary or regular	Special, rare and unique
Easily replaceable	Irreplaceable
Left around and passed around	Reserved for special occasions
Often placed on display for all to see	Kept in safe keeping often well protected

Now do you see what I mean? These are only a few distinctions between tools and jewels, yet it clearly shows which one we belong in when it comes to the two categories. When we get a clear understanding of who we are, and what we were created for it can transform our lives like never before. We can't allow the world to define who we are; instead we must define ourselves for the world.

Once we are clear, there will be certain things that are just plain unacceptable when it comes to how we treat ourselves and how we allow ourselves to be treated.

Tool Box or Jewelry Box?

Every day, we send a clear message to the world of what is acceptable and what is unacceptable. Whether intentionally or unintentionally, there is a message being communicated loud and clear.

When it comes to clothes, many girls often feel the shorter, tighter or lower cut, the better; often mistaking the looks, comments and attention from others (especially guys) as a sign of flattery and acceptance. But in reality what happens in most cases is that very same girl who was looking for attention is placed in the category of one of many tools in a tool box, instead of being placed in a Jewelry box as one who is special and set apart.

Got Ice Cream?

My family and I love ice cream. In fact, not a day goes by that we don't have a scoop or two. When it comes to the message we send daily, I am reminded of an analogy a friend of mine named Cliff Baskerville shares with youth in packed classrooms and auditoriums around the country about ice cream.

He often asks students, how many of them like ice cream. Well obviously, the hands go up as people begin to imagine their favorite flavors on a big, fat, crunchy cone.

He goes on asking them to imagine going to their favorite ice cream parlor with their mouths watering, to ask for their favorite flavor only to be told there is none available. If that wasn't enough, as they think of other flavors to substitute, they are told over and over again that there is none available. Can you imagine going to an ice cream parlor and there is NO ice cream of any flavor available? That would be wacky huh? Especially if the signs and advertisements clearly say "Ice Cream".

Well when it comes to the way many girls dress, they too are advertising but the message they are sending may be misleading. By all appearances, the short skirts, the tight pants and low-cut shirts are sending a message to the world. Now it may not be a good message or an accurate message of who they really are, but just like the ice cream parlor, when our sign says one thing, we shouldn't be surprised when people approach us in a specific manner.

Don't' get me wrong, I don't feel that anyone should ever be disrespected or violated in any way. However, I do feel that as Priceless GEMS we need to be intentional about the messages we project to the world through the clothes we wear, the things we say and the way we carry ourselves.

Not for sale

Do you measure up? Before you answer that question, first ask yourself, by what standard are you measuring yourself? Is it the world's standard or God's standard? Is it based on an unrealistic, false reality of a picture-perfect person created through marketing; or is it based on your personal, unique blueprint that was designed by the Creator of the universe before the beginning of time?

I'm not saying that all marketing and media is bad, however, when it comes to beauty magazines, commercials and advertisements, there are billions of dollars and countless hours spent behind the scenes, cutting, airbrushing, pasting and slimming down even the thinnest of models. Did you know…

- Advertisers spend $15-17 billion dollars a year directly on marketing to kids.
- By age 6, most kids can name more than 200 brands.
- Teens in the US spend approximately $160 billion a year.

I am going to go head and say, that kids and teenagers have a lot of buying power. It's no secret that companies spend big money on marketing to kids for a couple of reasons. One of the biggest reasons is so they can make lots of money and even build lifetime customers.

Companies want you to compare yourself to the stunning, flawless models in their advertisements. What they don't advertise is the fact that most of the pictures have been airbrushed or altered by computer programs, reducing certain parts of the body while enlarging other parts.

It's all in a master plan to get you to compare yourself to these images in an effort to get you to buy their products or services. Whether it is facial cream, makeup, hair products, jewelry or clothes, the implied message is always the same... "Our product will make you look or feel better and it will make life wonderful."   Usually there is also another implied message that says when you use our products or wear our brands, that others will like you or in some cases even love you. If you don't believe me, just take a minute to skim through a magazine or really watch or listen to the commercials.

Whatever it takes to make you feel less attractive and less equipped, makes it easier to get your mind and your money. Whether it is expensive advertisements or celebrity endorsements, companies will do what they have to do because at the end of the day it is all about dollars and cents.

The good news is that regardless of how much money they spend hyping their goods, you don't have to fall for the hype or be played like a puppet. You have an opportunity to begin to understand how media and marketing works, which can help empower you to recognize the tricks of the trade and not be brainwashed or fooled.

What you tolerate over time you will eventually begin to accept as normal. That's why it is important to ask yourself some questions when it comes to the things you see and hear.

The reality is that everything isn't good for everybody. This is true in many areas from, the music we listen to and the things we watch, to the books we read, to the things we put on, over and in our bodies. Not everything for sale or promoted today is meant for you. In fact, if the truth be told, some things may not be suitable for anyone.

When you watch television, listen to music, or see an advertisement, begin to ask yourself the following questions:

- *What is the company or artist trying to sell?*

- *Does this music/ad/product suggest that I have a problem or offer a solution to a problem* (example: "This product will remove zits.")?

- *How does the media make me feel about myself? Does it make me feel good about myself and build my confidence or does it leave me feeling that I need this product to improve myself?*

Is there anything you can do when it comes to impacting the media and the messages they communicate? Yes!

- Make your voice heard by writing to advertisers and let them know how you feel.

- Don't buy or support the products that send a negative message or a message that you don't agree with. Money talks louder than words in many instances.

- Support products, companies and artists that have positive messages.

- Share your view with your friends and teach them how to be smart consumers.

PRICELESS PRINCIPLE - #8

Remember you are a rare and precious Jewel. You were not created to be used and manipulated like a tool.

PRICELESS POINTERS
(ON SELF-RESPECT)

◈ Know who you are and walk in your power and purpose.

◈ Remember, you set the standard on how you are to be treated.

◈ Set boundaries. Know what you will and will not tolerate from others and stand firm.

◈ Know your value and make sure others know it by the way you carry yourself and the way you speak about yourself to others.

◈ NEVER lower your standards to gain "popularity".

◈ Be your own person, by understanding your value and setting the standard for what's acceptable and what's not, and NEVER sell yourself cheap or underestimate yourself or your ability to be all that you can be.

---⟨⟩---

Chapter 9
DIAMONDS ARE
A GIRL'S BEST FRIEND
(FRIENDSHIPS & HEALTHY RELATIONSHIPS)

Years ago there was a song called *Diamonds Are a Girls Best Friend.* While the lyrics were referring to real diamonds, the same is true when it comes to our lives and to people we call our friends. If we consider ourselves to be Priceless GEMS who are striving to shine brightly, then doesn't it make sense that we surround ourselves with others who feel the same way about themselves and about us?

Just think about it, would you find a real diamond ring in a jewelry showcase next to a bubble gum ring? Well why in the world would you surround yourself with fake, foolish and flaky people?

Let's be clear, I am not talking about selecting people based on their class, status or the things they possess. We've already come to the conclusion that those things are temporary anyway. Instead, I am talking about choosing to spend time with people who share your values, who encourage you to be your best, and who motivate you to be better and to do greater things than you've ever done before. Now with that in mind, when it comes to your best friends or those you spend the most time with, would you say they are a reflection of you?

Birds of a Feather

When I was younger, my grandparents used to say, "Birds of a feather flock together." In other words, you are just like the people you hang around. Just think about it for a minute, have you ever seen a chicken flying with the pigeons in the park? How about turkeys chilling out with the seagulls on the beach? My point is made. It simply doesn't happen.

When it comes to friendships it is very similar, although you and your friends don't have to be carbon copies of one another. You don't have to be the same race, from the same neighborhood or do everything together with your friends. However, it is important that you share similar values, have common interests and have a mutual respect for one another.

Values:

The moral principles and beliefs or accepted standards of a person or social group.

Our values affect our choices in life, so it's important to know what your values are and those of your friends. Although most people don't think that sharing the same values with your friends is a big deal, when it comes to choosing who to hang out with, it is one of the most important things to consider.

If your friends value education or have a high work ethic, chances are they won't be encouraging you to skip class or to slack off at work. If your friends believe in respecting their own bodies and carrying themselves in a respectable manner, then they won't encourage you to act out, hook up or disrespect your body with drugs, alcohol or pre-marital sex.

What type of people are you hanging around? If we did a roll call of your friends would you be proud of the people you spend the majority of your time with, or would you be embarrassed? Are you hanging around people who are making you bad or better?

Beware of Imitations

Unlike real diamonds that are rare and hand-picked, imitation (also known as fake) diamonds, are a dime a dozen. Where it takes time and patience to perfect a real diamond, an imitation diamond is usually mass produced and there is nothing special about them.

When it comes to selecting your real friends it may take time to find another diamond in the crowd, but don't worry and don't settle. If you don't fit neatly into boxes that other people have created for you, it's okay; you weren't created to fit in, you were created to stand out.

Diamonds Sharpen Diamonds

Just as the Word says in Proverbs 27:17, "As iron sharpens iron, so one man (person) sharpens another", the same is true for diamonds. Did you know that only a diamond can cut and shape another diamond? The tools used to cut a diamond and help mold it into its ideal form have diamond dust on the tip of the tools. Without the diamond edge, there would be no beautiful, shimmering, diamond.

A diamond can only sharpen another diamond when they come together. They actually feed off one another through their interaction, much like we do when it comes to those closest to us.

When it comes to our friends and those we allow in our life, they help to cut and shape us too. They can mold us with their words, their actions, their behaviors and attitudes for good or for bad. They can influence our values, the way we feel about ourselves, our dreams and our goals. Our friends either build us up or break us down. What do your friends do?

It is important to pick friends who inspire you to do great things. They should be positive people who uplift you and not people who bring you down with their words or by their mere presence. You know the ones I am talking about, the rude, selfish, hateful, back-biting, backstabbing, drama queens and kings.

It's always good to take time to evaluate your friendships from time to time. Sometimes you have friends who are around for a season and it is important to know when that season is over. Perhaps you used to have a lot in common with one another but then find that the older you get you find yourselves growing apart.

Maybe you have a friend who has changed her focus, gotten distracted or started making choices that aren't in line with your values. Perhaps she is not motivated and is not going in the direction that your life is taking. In those instances, there is no love lost, and it might be time to make some hard, fast decisions to change the nature of your friendship.

It's been said, "People come into your life for a reason, a season or a lifetime". We harm ourselves when we try to hold onto relationships that have come to an end. When we find ourselves in that place, it's always best to recognize it, let go and move on.

You want to know something deep? Not everyone is going where you are going. There are some who will choose not to go based on their choices. Others won't go because they don't believe they can go. Lastly, there are some who won't go where you are going just because they are plain lazy.

They may not understand that each one of us is priceless and created for a specific purpose. Don't allow yourself to miss an incredible future because you were caught up hanging with imitations instead of the real thing. It would be like having an opportunity to select between a genuine diamond or a piece of costume jewelry. Why settle for less, when you can have God's very best?

Diamond Makers & Diamond Breakers

Growing up today can be challenging with all the pressures of life. Pressures from parents, teachers, friends and society in general can make it difficult and create a challenge for any girl. But, did you know that not all pressure is bad?

Diamonds are actually formed under enormous pressure which is essential when it comes to it being transformed from a rough rock to a radiant gem. When it comes to our lives, some of life's pressures can crush us or add unnecessary stress, almost to the point where it seems unbearable. Then there is other pressure in life that can be used to make us better and help us shine brighter.

Diamond Breakers

In order to be the best you can be it is important to be selective in the people you hang around and the people you allow to impact your life. There will be people who build you up and others whose main mission is to break you down.

In most schools and even in our own families, we can often have what I call Diamond Breakers. They are the people who can often hurt you the most by the way they shoot down your ideas, make fun of you in different ways, or do other things that cause you to spend more time wondering why and working to make things better.

Diamond Breakers are often people who don't know their own value and, in many cases, are intimidated by or jealous of the value and potential they see in you. They disguise themselves as friends to get close to you and to earn your trust, but their words and actions are often more harmful than helpful.

I once heard it said that people are like elevators; they either take you up or take you down. Make sure the people in your life lift you up instead of bringing you down.

A wise woman named Xernonia Clayton once said, "If you can't change the people you are around...then change the people you are around." In other words, if you find yourself surrounded by Diamond Breakers who are unwilling to change for the better, then it's up to you to pick some other people to hang around.

You can't change the way other people think or act, but what you can change is the people you allow to shape and mold you.

Diamond Makers

There will be other people in your life I call Diamond Makers. These are positive people who love you unconditionally and who truly want the best for you. Every GEM needs a few Diamond Makers in her life. Whether it is a family member, your favorite teacher, best friend or your mentor, it is important to have someone you can go to and who keeps it real without judgment or ridicule. Diamond Makers are people who are honest with you and who push you to be the best you can be.

It's a great day to do an inventory of your friendships and associations. Ask yourself, are the people closest to you

 Diamond Makers or Diamond Breakers? If you determine that you have some Diamond Breakers in your camp, get them out as soon as possible. The longer they hang around, the more damage they can cause.

If you find as you go down your list of friends, that you don't

have many Diamond Makers, the first thing I would suggest is to simply open your eyes. Often times, they are right in front of us, and they may be easily overlooked or even taken for granted. They may even be people who, until today, we considered too hard, too strict and too tough. But again, it's usually these very same people who recognize our value and potential and see more in us than we may see in ourselves.

Could it really be true, that those family members and friends who give us such a hard time, create crazy rules and nag all the time, actually don't want to make our life miserable, but instead want the very best for us? You better believe it!!!

Having Patience Through the Process

What kind of people do you hang out with? Who are you allowing to speak into your life and influence you? Can you think of some Diamond Makers in your life who are always pushing you, correcting you or encouraging you every day to be better? Sometimes, it feels good to know someone is in your corner, but at other times it can be a bit annoying.

For instance, when your parents, teachers, mentors or those who want the best for you are constantly on you to study hard and to maintain good grades, or maybe they are picky and critical about the people you hang out with, do you tune them out?

It may seem like they are going overboard and making a big deal out of nothing, but in most cases they can see something in you that maybe you can't see in yourself. On top of that, many of them have been where you are and made choices that they still have the emotional and sometimes physical scars to show for their decisions.

Your parents aren't called your guardians for nothing. They are supposed to "guard" you and guide you through life, so take note. The adults in your life may not have all the answers, but I'm sure they have many answers about life and can help you avoid some of the mistakes and emotional and physical experiences in life.

But guess what? No one can live your life for you. You've got to want God's best for your life and be willing to do what you've got to do to get it.

Sometimes when the pressure is on it's natural to want to run and hide, but I've learned over the years, that it's better to face things head on, otherwise you are bound to find yourself in the same or similar situations again in the future.

Remember, even though you are young, it doesn't mean you can't be wise. Listen, ask questions when you don't understand, make a commitment to yourself to make good choices and to withstand the negative pressures of life and to embrace the positive things in life.

PRICELESS PRINCIPLE - #9

Remember to surround yourself with Diamond Makers and stay clear of all Diamond Breakers.

PRICELESS POINTERS
(ON FRIENDSHIPS & HEALTHY RELATIONSHIPS)

❖ Pick friends who allow you to be yourself and who accept you unconditionally.

❖ The people you hang around will either affect your life or infect your life.

❖ Surround yourself with people of like minds and positive attitudes, who share your morals and values.

❖ Find an accountability partner, someone you can really trust to help you monitor the things you say and do.

❖ Keep it positive and keep it real. Life is too short for playing around so look to those who will always tell you the truth (in love) because they have YOUR best interests at heart.

Chapter 10
A BRILLIANT MIND
(SELF-CONFIDENCE)

You are a "Brillionaire". Yes, I said a "Brillionaire", which, if you didn't know means someone rich in good ideas or a person with many good plans or ideas. It's not enough to simply have good ideas, so the question becomes what are you doing with them? To have great ideas but to never do anything with them is like having a rare, beautiful diamond that you keep hidden in a box and keep to yourself, versus placing it on your finger for the world to see.

Author Ken Gaub says, "Each person's mind is a billion-dollar gift from God. No computer can match its capabilities. God made our minds for a purpose...Just like a computer we make decisions and draw conclusions from the material we feed into our mind."

This is why it is important to guard your gates and to be careful what you allow to enter your mind and your thoughts. You are what you think, from your head down to your feet. Our thoughts guide our lives for better or for worse. Whether we realize it or not, what we think influences what we do.

Success doesn't just fall from the sky onto your head; you do things that place you on the path to success. You will never change the way things are in your life until you change the way you think. It's only then that you will change the way you do things, and as a result, your future changes.

Take time on a regular basis to analyze your thoughts and think about what you are thinking about. When it comes to your thoughts, there are four simple steps that are easy to remember.

#1 - Face It

Begin by facing or acknowledging what you think or feel. So often we lie to ourselves and others about our true feelings and thoughts. You can't fix what's broken until you first recognize and acknowledge that it's broken.

Example: A girl who thinks to herself 'I am so fat and ugly'.

#2 - Trace It

Next, it's important to trace where that thought came from. Ask yourself if that thought was planted by something you heard or something you saw. Or perhaps, it is what you have always thought about the matter based on what you learned from experience or growing up.

Example: Maybe the girl thinks she is fat and ugly because she was teased as a child by her older brother and mean kids at school.

#3 - Erase It

If you realize that the thought is negative then take a bold step and begin to erase it mentally from your mind.

Example: A girl begins to remove negative lies in her head by not saying or playing those words over and over again in her mind.

#4 - Replace It

And last of all, once you face it, trace it and erase it, it is vitally important that you replace that negative thought with a positive thought.

Example: A girl replaces the lies she has been playing over and over in her head with the truth that she was created beautiful, unique and full of potential.

Inner Strength

One thing about diamonds is they are one of the hardest substances on earth. In fact, the root word for diamond means unconquerable. I mention that to merely remind you of your own strength because it takes strength and courage to stand for what you believe, especially if what you believe is different than what is popular.

You have to be willing to stand for your own values and beliefs even if you have to stand alone. I once heard a quote that summarized it all, "People can't stand by you, until they know where you stand."

You have to learn to think for yourself which means you also have to know why you believe something. In an era of information overload, everyone on earth has an opinion about something. It's not enough to base your opinion or take a stand for something because your friends are doing it or because you saw something on television or read it on the internet.

Because there is so much information at your fingertips today and so many different media outlets, it is important to research the facts on issues through reliable sources so you can formulate your own opinions and be willing and able to stand for what you feel or believe.

You have to take time to expand your mind so that you are able to take a stand based on facts, whether about a hot topic in the news, a social or political issue, or your faith. It's important to know why you believe something and why you choose to do or not do something.

Once you are able to develop the ability to think for yourself and to set boundaries and standards for yourself, you will find it becomes much easier to stand up to negative peer pressure and outside influences. You may find yourself with new friends or in some cases few friends, but don't let that scare you. In the end, it's well worth it

Character Counts

What are your values? What is important to you and why? Have you set standards for yourself that you are unwilling to compromise, or are you moved by your emotions or what everyone around you is doing? There is an old quote that says, "If you don't know what you stand for, you will fall for anything."

One way to make good choices and to stay on track is to determine your values and your personal goals and stay focused on those things. When you know what you believe and why you believe it, it makes it more difficult for others to sway you from your values.

When you are faced with tough choices that put your values to the test, it is most important to stay true to yourself. Whether it is lying, cheating, hanging with the wrong crowd, or doing something your parents don't approve of, it is always important to think about how your choices would compare or line up to the values deep within your heart.

It is equally as important to control your thoughts, your words and to watch the people you hang around. All of these things play a significant role in the choices you make.

If your thoughts aren't pure or positive, then your actions won't be either. Every choice, good or bad, begins first with a thought. If you can get into the habit of choosing your thoughts then you can begin to change your actions. What do I mean by that? Well I'll give you an example. If you have an assignment in school on a subject you find challenging and you immediately think to yourself, "There is no way I am going to be able to complete this assignment", be careful. Chances are that thought will take root and before you know it you will begin saying out loud, "I'm going to fail this assignment, it's too hard for me, there is no way I can pass no matter how hard I try..." Naturally with that attitude, chances are you will not only fail the assignment but you may even fail the class.

Now imagine, if in that same situation you think to yourself, "Wow, this is a challenge but I know I can do this. It may be difficult but I'm thankful I have time to get it done and to ask for the help needed. I know if I have problems, I still have time to ask my teacher for additional help. I will make a good grade on this assignment because I am going to apply myself." Do you see the difference? Just changing your thinking can have a profound effect on the outcome.

Frank Outlaw is quoted as saying, "Watch your actions, they become your habits. Watch your habits, they become your character. Watch your character, it becomes your destiny."

PRICELESS PRINCIPLE - #10

*Remember to be willing to stand for what you
believe, even if it means you have to stand alone.*

PRICELESS POINTERS
(ON SELF-CONFIDENCE)

◈ Remember self-confidence is not something you are born with, but something you have to develop over time.

◈ Begin to encourage and affirm yourself daily with your thoughts and words.

◈ Understand that confidence is different from conceit.

◈ Determine what you can do very well and begin to master your gift by practicing it regularly.

◈ Try doing something new. Specifically something you used to tell yourself you couldn't do.

Chapter 11
SET APART
(SELF-ASSURANCE)

Being a Priceless GEM can be lonely at times. One of the great things about a diamond is the fact that it can stand alone. Although often accompanied by other gems or jewels, the reality is that a diamond is complete all by itself, and in many cases may be even more stunning and breathtaking when it stands alone.

The word "independent" means to stand alone and not to be dependent on another's opinion. As a Priceless GEM, it is important to maintain your independence when it comes to the ways and influences of the world. Just as an expensive diamond is often kept in a display case for safety, protection and safekeeping, you have to be willing to be set apart and to protect yourself in a similar manner.

There are a lot things battling for your attention. If you are not careful, it's easy to become dependent on other people or to be more concerned with what other people are doing or what they think than on what is important to you. If you are not careful you can live your whole life trying to be what some call a "people pleaser", and as a former people pleaser, I am here to tell you that's a miserable way to live. Trying to get the approval of others is exhausting.

If I had only known when I was younger what I know today, I could have saved myself a lot of sleepless nights, heartache and wasted time and energy. I have learned through trial and error how important it is to be truly comfortable in the skin you are in.

This means you have to set standards for yourself and not allow the media, your friends or anyone else to set them for you. The opinion of others and what is popular changes like the wind. In fact, I often say, people change their opinions on what's popular like they change their underwear. If you spend your time basing your value on the latest styles, being popular and liked by others or any of these types of things, you will soon find yourself either worn out or outdated like yesterday's news.

You weren't created to fit in, you were created to **STAND OUT!**

If you are smart you won't waste your time trying to measure up to these things, but instead will focus your time and attention on being a person of integrity and purpose. Embrace the fact that you are set apart. There should be something distinctively different about you. You are a precious GEM, a Priceless treasure.

Handle With Care

Most expensive diamonds are often kept safe under lock and key and are only brought out or worn for special occasions. They are rarely passed around, loaned out or handled carelessly. In fact, it's the total opposite. They are typically handled with care and set apart. It's no secret that whatever we determine to be valuable, we guard and protect and handle with care.

Imagine you were given a gift of precious diamonds worth over $50,000. Can you picture yourself wearing them to the local grocery store to pick up a gallon of milk or a pack of toilet paper? Would you let your friend borrow them to wear as they hang out and chill? No need to answer, because I know you are saying, "Of course not".

I think you would agree that it would be foolish to wear expensive jewelry just anywhere or lend them out to anyone even if you trusted them. Well, just like you wouldn't be careless with your expensive jewelry or take it any and everywhere, as Priceless GEMS you can't allow yourself to go everywhere, do everything and allow any and everyone to handle, or in some cases, to mishandle you.

Can you think of a couple of places that you shouldn't go, or a few people you really shouldn't hang around? Maybe there are people who try to pressure you to do things you don't want to do, or maybe they influence you to act in ways that are not appropriate.

Are you comfortable with choices you are making in life? Can you honestly say that your closest friends make good choices and encourage you to do the same? Are you feeling pressured to do things that make you feel uncomfortable? Are you tempted to follow the crowd instead of following God and His plan and purpose for your life? These are just a few of the hard questions that only you can answer.

What's a girl to do? How in the world can you withstand the pressure and avoid these types of situations and people? Well, I'm glad you asked. It first begins by recognizing your own value. If you don't value yourself, why in the world would you expect anyone else to?

It's pretty simple. We teach people how to treat us based on the way we think about ourselves and the way we act. The way we see ourselves often affects the way others see us and even treat us. Now there are a few exceptions. I am not speaking of being a victim in situations of abuse beyond our ability to control, like rape,

> *If you don't value yourself, why in the world should you expect anyone else to?*

molestation or other forms of abuse. If anything like this has ever happened to you, please know it is not your fault. There is never a justified reason for someone to violate another person, regardless of the circumstances.

But, when it comes to our behavior, our words, our attitude and the way we carry ourselves, all send a strong message. It's a message of confidence and being self-assured, or it's a message of uncertainty and self-doubt.

What do your words and actions say about you? If someone were to listen to you or observe you from afar, would your words and actions say that you respect yourself and others? Would they determine you are a person of integrity and good character or would they assume otherwise? Would they see you as a good friend and a person who could be trusted, or would your words and actions reveal you to be a gossiping, insecure, backstabbing hater? Would your actions and words set you apart as a leader or would they indicate that you are a follower through and through?

If you find that maybe you need to do a better job of lining your words, thoughts and actions up with your values, then good for you. The reason I say good is because you can't begin to change something until you first recognize there is a problem.

It is something that you will have to focus on and make an effort to do daily and it's as simple as asking yourself those same questions and making the proper changes. The more you do it, the easier it will become.

Beware of Thieves

Because you are priceless and full of value and potential, it is important that you be watchful; staying on guard when it comes to thieves. If you are not careful you could be totally robbed of your destiny.

There is a real enemy in the world and he isn't wearing a dark mask and trench coat. He is lurking and seeking an opportunity to strike and steal your joy, your peace, your body, your mind and your future. You name it; if it is good, he is looking for a way to snatch it.

The Word of God says, "The thief comes to steal, kill and destroy, but I came so that you might have life and to the full until it overflows"- John 10:10.

The enemy is looking for opportunities to get you distracted and off track. If he can get you off focus and trip you up, he can steal your destiny and the very thing God sent you to this earth to do. This is not meant to scare you, but instead to make you aware, and to equip you to make better choices and to be on guard.

Staying On Guard

Thieves often conduct a stakeout to study their victims before they attack, and the enemy is no different. He is checking us out

to see if there are areas where he can creep in and take over.

So how does he actually do it? Is he crafty and sneaky or is he bold in his approach? Well I'm glad you asked. The enemy doesn't walk through our front door and literally snatch our futures from underneath us. Instead, he uses things like our bad habits and poor attitudes to get us off track. Things like the following:

- **A Sense of Entitlement** – feeling you have a right to something or feeling that something is owed to you.

- **Indecisiveness** – being unable to make a decision.

- **Idleness** – being unfocused, unproductive and not having any real purpose in doing something.

- **Laziness** – being slow and sluggish. Not wanting to work hard.

- **Making Excuses** – not taking responsibility for your actions.

- **Jealousy & Envy** – being unhappy or having angry feelings of wanting to have what someone else has.

- **Procrastination** – putting important tasks off until a later time.

- **Regret** – feeling sad or sorry about (something that you did or did not do).

- **Unhealthy Friendships or Relationships** – associating with people who negatively impact your life.

Now that you know some of the methods the enemy uses, you can be on the lookout and do everything possible to avoid those traps.

- Acknowledge those areas where you are weak and get help and support as needed.

- Be intentional on how you spend your time.

- Be selective about the music you listen to, the TV and movies you watch, and the conversations you have.

- Get an accountability partner who will encourage you and help you get on track and stay on track.

PRICELESS PRINCIPLE - #11
Remember, you were not made to fit in…
You were made to Stand Out.

PRICELESS POINTERS
(ON SELF-ASSURANCE)

💎 Set standards for yourself and don't allow the media, your friends or anyone else to set them for you.

💎 Maintain your independence when it comes to the ways and influences of the world.

💎 Stand for what you believe, even if you have to stand alone.

💎 Guard your gates and protect your heart.

Chapter 12
CREATED WITH CLASS
(SELF-EXPRESSION · FASHION & IMAGE)

To get respect you have to first believe that you deserve it. You have to walk with respect, talk with respect, and carry yourself in a manner which demands respect.

Years ago a talented artist named Lauryn Hill released a song called *DooWop* (also known as *That Thing*) which had a line that said, "Why be a hard rock when you really are a gem?" Even though that song was produced decades ago, that question remains the same today.

Having an opportunity to work with thousands of girls over the years, I am seeing more and more who are doing everything in their power to look, act, and sound harder than ever before. The interesting thing is that no matter how aggressive they act or how loudly they talk, at the end of the day everyone is left shaking their head and wondering, "What in the world is up with her?"

We have all seen the girl, or group of girls, talking or laughing so loudly that it annoys everyone around. Or how about the girl who is like a drama magnet, always finding herself in the middle of some ridiculous situation? And then there are the foul-mouthed girls who cuss so much that it would make a grown man embarrassed.

When we don't value ourselves, it will without a doubt show in the way we act, the way we dress, the words we speak, the way we carry ourselves and the way we allow others treat us. As a Priceless GEM you have always got to be aware of the way you conduct yourself.

Just as a diamond is a diamond at all times, as a Priceless GEM you should carry yourself accordingly at all times. Carrying yourself with class is a learned behavior, but please understand, there is a difference between being a young woman with class versus being a snob.

As a Priceless Gem, when you walk into the room, the atmosphere should change...for the better. Not because you talk loudly, are really flashy or demand attention in some form or fashion, but simply because you are present.

Modesty Matters

Many girls find themselves so busy following the latest fashion trends and trying to keep up with the designs of the day that they often loose their individuality and a clear sense of who they are in the process. Instead of allowing their individuality and personality to shine through, they begin to blend into the crowd.

If that isn't enough, they can allow the fashions of the day to cause them to contradict and compromise their values, allowing their outer appearance to send a message that is totally opposite of who they really are.

We are living in a world that says less is best and skin is in. The tighter, the shorter, the more revealing the clothes, the better, but don't get sucked into believing that lie.

When it comes to being a real young woman of distinction, the reality is that modesty still matters. What is modesty you ask? Modesty means, to dress, act and speak in a manner that is respectable, decent and in order. In other words, not allowing your style of dress or the way you carry yourself to express anything less than the fact that you are a young lady of value and class.

There is absolutely nothing wrong with being a fashionable young lady, as long as you understand that you make the clothes, the clothes don't make you.

When it comes to clothes, do you dress to impress? Do you have to have the latest and greatest designer clothes, shoes and accessories in order to keep up? Does the way that you dress on the outside reflect your values on the inside? Do you dress to draw attention and turn heads? Well, I regret to inform you that none of those

reflect your status as a Priceless GEM. Instead, they can lead to you selling yourself short and setting yourself up for regret.

A Walking Billboard

Take a ride in any major city, and you will find billboards advertising everything imaginable. From soft drinks, to clothing, to local services, all the billboards along city streets are communicating a message and they are also seeking a response.

Whether we realize it or not, each one of us is a walking billboard. The clothes we wear, the way we carry ourselves and the things that come out of our mouths also communicate a message. Knowing that, what do your clothes say about you? Do you dress for yourself or for the response that you will receive from others? Many girls select clothes to get attention from guys. They secretly feel powerful because of the reaction and responses they generate from others.

When it comes to your clothes and whether something is appropriate or not, simply ask yourself, "What does this outfit say about me?"

Are your pants so tight that your body parts are hanging over the side? Is your skirt so short that you can't sit down comfortably without tugging at your skirt to pull it down? How about your shirts? Are they too tight or low cut?

How about you? Do you dress for the attention you get from others? Honestly answer that question for yourself as you move forward.

Let's face it, it can be flattering to have people comment favorably about an outfit or hairstyle. However, when we start dressing, selecting or buying clothes, strictly based on what people say and think, that's a problem.

Clothes & Fashion

Most girls like to dress up and look nice, and I don't expect you to be any different. However, as a Priceless GEM you must be sure to remember that you make the clothes and the clothes don't make you. What that means is to not get caught up in the latest or greatest fashion. So many get caught up in that, only to learn that they can never catch up because what's hot is forever changing.

Instead, it's better to determine for yourself what you like and what looks best on you. You need to begin by thinking about things like which colors best compliment you. Believe it or not, most people have colors that are more becoming on them than others. Depending on your hair or eye color, or maybe the complexion of your skin, there may be some colors that are more flattering than others.

The next thing you need to take into consideration when it comes to clothes is your body type. Like we discussed earlier, each one of us is unique in design but each one of us is fabulous in our own right.

In most cases when you see the fashion magazines, they have created through software and special effects what appears to be the perfect body, but in reality, that is so far from real life or real people.

Because of that, we tend to see girls and women in clothing that doesn't fit properly and in many cases may be downright offensive. You know what I'm talking about. I'm sure you have seen someone a time or two and thought to yourself, "What was she thinking?" We've all seen that, and many of us may have even been that girl. But the great thing is it's never too late to make a change for the positive.

So in order to avoid being that girl, we begin with knowing our body type and which styles and colors compliment us best. Notice, I didn't say anything about knowing what styles were hot, or what everyone else is wearing. I see so many people spending so much time trying to impress others that they lose themselves in the process and get to a point where they don't remember who they are or even what they like.

Be a trendsetter instead of a trend tracker.

I'm going to tell you as I tell others, "Be true and do you". In other words, be true to yourself first and foremost, and don't allow others to dictate who you can, will and should be in life.

Tips on Dressing

Below are just a few simple tips that all Priceless GEMS can use when it comes to dressing:

- **Keep your underwear under wraps** - In other words, underwear should be worn but not seen. There is nothing like seeing a girl whose bra straps or panties are creeping out under their clothes. Make sure your underwear is not shown to the world and remember it's called "under" wear for a reason.

- **Cover your crack** - All cracks must remain covered at all times. It may sound funny but it's true. Don't you dare walk out of the house with your pants so low that your butt is showing. Nor is it cool to leave the house with your shirt so low cut that cleavage is all you see.

- **Just because they sell it doesn't mean you should buy it** - It's not okay to follow the trends and fads if the items don't fit or they take away from the image you want to project. Remember that you make the clothes, the clothes and brands don't make you. With that said, pick clothes that complement your body shape and size and represents the message and image you want to portray.

- **Layer up** - Showing skin is NOT in, no matter what you think. Learn how to layer your clothing so your cleavage, your stomach and your butt crack aren't showing.

- **Know your size** - This means you can't always borrow your best friend's clothes, because you two may be two different sizes. From bras to bottoms, it is important to know your correct size. Also, consider buying slightly larger sizes for items meant to have a tight fit.

- **Finger Tip Test** - In schools all over the nation, they have implemented what is referred to as the Finger Tip Test. It's a great way to determine if a skirt is too short. It's a really simple test you can do when you have on a skirt by allowing your hands to fall at your side. If your fingertips are longer than the end of your skirt, then chances are your skirt is too short.

  You may be wondering "What's the big deal?", but we have all seen girls who have to bend over or had the wind blow and all their goods are exposed for the world to see. Let me be the first to tell you, there is nothing cute, attractive or fashionable about that at all.

- **Own it** - If you are reading this book chances are you dress yourself so remember...it's on you! It's your responsibility to determine how you present yourself to the world.

It's not about coming up with a long list of rules that you have to follow or else, but it is about reminding you that your body is valuable and is to be treasured and not placed on display for the entire world to see. Modesty does matter, especially in a world where everything and anything goes. Take pride in the way you dress and in the way you carry yourself. Many times it speaks much louder than any words you could ever say.

Assertiveness vs. Aggressiveness

Part of being a Priceless GEM, is being clear about what you want in any given situation and knowing how to go about getting it. It's important to understand the difference between being assertive and being aggressive.

Being assertive is having a plan and putting it into action while presenting your best foot forward and respecting others. It's about knowing what you want and how to get it in a non-threatening or non-hostile way. Getting what you want doesn't mean walking over others.

Being aggressive is to totally disregard others by selfishly and forcefully going after what you want. It means saying and doing things that may be viewed as hostile, unfriendly, combative, intimidating, and otherwise offensive.

Always stand up for yourself, but learn to be confident, bold and assertive without being aggressive and offensive. You've got a voice and it's important to use it.

A Few Brilliant Basics

If you want to be treated like a lady, you have to act like a lady, and part of being a lady is "representing" at all times. As a Priceless GEM, there are a few things which I refer to as Brilliant Basics that every girl must follow.

- **Eye Contact** - Practice looking people in their eyes when you speak to them. Looking people in the eyes is a sign of confidence. Don't stare them down or try to make them feel uncomfortable.

- **Hand Out & Head Up** - Give a firm handshake when being introduced or introducing yourself to others.

- **Act Like You Know** - Conduct yourself in a manner that communicates that you know who you are.

- **Inside Voice** - Watch your tone when you speak. Don't yell at or over people. Part of effective communication is remembering you don't have to be loud to be heard and you don't interrupt others while they are speaking.

- **Less is Best** - When it comes to make-up. Remember make-up is created to enhance God's beauty, not cover it up. If you and your family decide that you can wear make-up, learn how to properly apply it and select colors and tones that compliment you instead of covering up.

- **Nail Check** - If you know me, you know this is one of my big rules. NO chipped polish allowed! If you wear nail polish make sure to keep it together. This means if it is chipping, take if off or touch it up. This rule also goes for your toes too.

- **Show That You Care** - Show respect to others rather than trying to keep the spotlight on you.

I really wish girls had a clue about the power they possess. Through our actions, our words and the way we carry ourselves, we often teach others how to treat us. In most cases, what we wear sets the tone for how we want to be treated. Now this does not mean that if you dress respectfully that there might not be an ignorant guy who will still approach you inappropriately. However, the clothes we wear and the things we say combine to send a message. The question is, is it the right message?

Extraordinary

At a glance you may appear to be normal or blend in with the crowd, but in actuality there is hidden potential that, with a few final touches, could be the difference in you blending in and standing out. You may think that you are just an ordinary girl, but God didn't make you ordinary, He created you to be "Extraordinary".

Extraordinary:

*To be extraordinary means to be remarkable,
and beyond what is ordinary or usual.*

Unlike costume jewelry, which people tend to throw around and handle any kind of way, diamonds are different. Most real diamonds are kept in jewelry boxes and only brought out on special occasions. The owners recognize their value and handle them with the utmost care; not even allowing their closest friends and family to play around with or mishandle them.

Well, the same should be true for us. I see so many beautiful young girls, who are true diamonds, yet they don't realize their value, and because of that they allow others to mishandle them or treat them like anything other than the Priceless GEM they are.

When ordinary people decide to do extraordinary things, they transform their lives and the lives of others around them."

— Oprah Winfrey

You may not get to do everything everyone else is doing, but remember that you are going places that everyone is not going. You weren't meant to fit in. Instead, you were created to stand out, because like a diamond you are remarkable, full of beauty and created for a purpose.

Are you allowing yourself to be influenced by the media to act and dress in provocative ways in clothing that is inappropriate, or allowing boys to talk to or handle you physically with no respect?

There is a powerful quote from Oprah Winfrey that reads, *"When ordinary people decide to do extraordinary things, they transform their lives and the lives of others around them."*

It's important for girls to take a stand and open their eyes to recognize that they are a treasure beyond measure. We can't expect others to treat us with respect if our actions and words scream that we don't respect ourselves.

PRICELESS PRINCIPLE - #12

Your body is valuable and is to be treasured and not placed on display for the entire world to see.

PRICELESS POINTERS
(ON SELF-EXPRESSION - FASHION & IMAGE)

- Love the skin you are in.

- Remind yourself that you were not created ordinary, you were created EXTRAORDINARY!!!

- Be true and do you!!!

- Become comfortable with your body shape and seek styles that best compliment your figure.

Chapter 13
MAINTAINING CLARITY
(SELF-DISCIPLINE – GOAL SETTING & ATTITUDE)

In order to reach your goals in life you first need to create some. It sounds silly doesn't it? But I find it quite disturbing to see hundreds and thousands of people aimlessly living life. Yes, they may have lofty goals of one day making a lot of money or retiring young to an exotic island, but because they have no plan for how to get there, it's nothing more than a pipe dream.

Write the Vision

So why don't people make goals? That's a good question. It may be because it takes time and it also requires focus. It takes time to actually think about what you want in life and then to begin to create a plan to get you there. After you come up with the plan it's only a mere thought until you actually write it down. The Bible says, "Write the vision, and make it plain so the heralds can run with it" - Habakkuk 2:2.

Next it takes honesty to look at where you are, figure out where you want to go, and then create a plan of action.

Sometimes this process can be painful or make your dreams seem impossible. The good news is with each step you take, you are getting closer and closer to your goal.

What do you want in life? What will it take to get you there? How will you stay focused? These are just a few of the questions you need to begin to consider and answer. Don't be fooled into thinking that you are still young and have the rest of your life ahead. Yes, you might be young, but your clock started ticking the day you were born.

Dreaming in Color

I am a big dreamer and always have been. I am not talking about the types of dreams that you have when you go to sleep and are slobbering all over your pillow, but I am talking about the type of dreaming you do in your heart and in your mind.

My Mom tells me that when I was a kid I used to say, "Mom, I'm dreaming with my eyes open". I wasn't old enough to understand that what I was doing was visualizing and seeing things I wanted to have and do. Would you consider yourself to be a dreamer? Do you dream with your eyes open? Do you dream in color?

When it comes to your life and to your future, I encourage you to dream in color. Not just in regular color but in HD color. The details of your dreams should be so vivid that it engages all your senses. Why do you think dreaming about your future is important? Well, we already determined earlier that all things begin first with a thought. If you aren't creating a dream and vision for your life, then you may find yourself living in someone else's dream, and instead of being the main character you will be an extra.

It's not enough just to dream about it, you have got to be about it. You have to write a plan and work your plan. You should aim to live your life the way you wrote it. It's not to say that things won't happen, but with a plan, it's much easier to get back on track at any point that you find yourself lost or off-course.

While we are talking about dreams and visions, let me ask, are you following your own dream or someone else's dream for your life? It could be a dream that someone else like your friends, family or others have created for you. That is one way you can find yourself living someone else's dream, but there is another way too.

People will often say, I want to be the next… you can fill in the blank with just about anyone's name. Whether they want to be the next Oprah Winfrey, the next Tyra Banks or the next BeYonce' doesn't really matter. You know why, because we will never be able to be someone else. It's okay to admire someone's talent or skills and to have role models that you admire, but to be the next whoever means that you would be living someone else's dream.

If you aren't currently a dreamer, I double dare you to start dreaming today. You can do this by simply closing your eyes and beginning to ask yourself about the type of life you want. Go a step further and think about who's in your dream with you encouraging and supporting you. Next, think about how your life is impacting those around you in a positive way. Make sure your dreams are not about what you can get, but about what you can give to others and to the world.

As you begin to visualize your life, take it a step further and write your dreams down in a journal or create a vision board with pictures, words and quotes. You can easily post your vision board on the wall in your room, or put it in your notebook or next to your calendar. The whole purpose is to keep it in front of you so it can serve as a constant reminder.

Do Things in Excellence

This seems rather elementary, but unfortunately today, things that used to be considered common sense aren't that common anymore. With the simple conveniences of life, we have become a lazy society that in many cases just does the bare minimum to get by. But as a Priceless GEM, the bare minimum is not enough nor is it acceptable.

Average people and average things don't stand out at all. In fact they are easily overlooked or forgotten altogether. Just think about it. When is the last time you remembered an average meal or an average movie? But along the same line, if I asked you to tell me the best meal you've had in the last month or the best movie you have ever seen, you would easily be able to tell me all about it.

It is important to strive to do all things in excellence. I am not talking about doing things perfectly, but doing them in excellence to the best of our ability. From your homework assignments to your chores around the house, give them all you've got.

Whiner or a Winner?

You may be thinking, yeah, but... I don't have... I can't do... It's not fair... and the excuses can go on and on and on. Yes, you might have different circumstances or challenges from the next girl. Your family may have faced challenges that are different from your friends. You may have some physical, emotional or financial limitations that create challenges in your life. While all of that may be true, it doesn't mean you can't achieve the things God has in store for you.

When it comes to excuses, Benjamin Franklin said, "He that is good for making excuses is seldom good for anything else."

Don't allow your thoughts and your mouth to hold you back or keep you bound. You are not responsible for what you don't have but you are responsible to use what you do have, and in this case you have been given a brilliant mind, a strong voice and the ability to make things happen.

You can choose to do what you can do with a positive attitude, or you can choose to whine and complain and stay right where you are...the choice is yours.

You can change many things about your life by simply changing your way of thinking and your habits. What things would you like to change in your life? Your grades? Your friends? Your relationship with your parents? Your attitude? Well, whatever it is, the first step in winning in these areas is to look at your attitude.

We should never let what we can't do, stop us from doing what we can do. We simply need to line our attitude up with our actions and move forward.

Our attitude can often speak louder than our words. Our attitude is a reflection of what we are thinking and they show up in spite of what we say. Our attitude is reflected in our facial expressions, our words, our tone, our body language and more. What does your attitude say about you?

Another thing about attitudes is they can often be contagious. I know you can think of someone who can walk into a room and change the whole atmosphere for the better or for the worse. I know you can also think of someone you have been around whose attitude has rubbed off on you in a positive or negative way.

> *Attitudes are contagious. Ask yourself is yours worth catching?*

As Priceless GEMS we need to remember that we are responsible for our own attitudes and for the energy we bring into a space with our attitudes. I am sure you have heard the phrase, "Your attitude determines your altitude"; well it's true.

In Search of Significance

God is searching for young people who will transform the world. You must be thinking there is no way you could do that, but the reality is that you can.

Do you desire to be successful or significant? That's an important question every Priceless GEM must ask herself. To be successful is great and can lead to a long list of achieved goals and accolades from others, but to be a person of significance is so much more meaningful. There are long lists of people who are successful from all outward appearances. In fact the list is likely too long to name, but many of those people are unhappy; absolutely hating life. From the outside, they have it all, the money, material stuff, and all the things the world says are important, but they are miserable because they have no clue about their purpose. What a sad existence.

It doesn't have to be that way for you. The choice is yours. You can choose to be

Change your goal from being the best in the world to being the best for the world.

someone who soars beyond success to a place of signifance, actually making a difference in the world. Again it calls for a shift in our thinking. We must change our goal from being the best in the world to focusing on being the best FOR the world.

It's been said that, the two most important days in a person's life are the day they were born and the day they find out why they were born. I dare you to seek that out. Believe me, when you figure that out, even at a young age, it will make life so much more fulfilling.

I dare you to begin living your life on purpose. You might be wondering what in the world I mean by that. I mean be intentional in the things you do, even if it is something as simple as doing your homework. Don't just do it because the teacher gave you the assignment, but focus your attention on what you're doing and do it purposefully to expand your mind and to get the top grade.

The world is searching for young people like you who will help to transform the world. You may be thinking there is no way you could do that, but believe it or not, you can. You have a unique mix of gifts, talents, abilities and ideas like no one else. Who knows, you could be the one to find a cure for AIDS or one day end world hunger. I dare you to get passionate about life and about your purpose in life.

Get Your "But" Out The Way

What is your "but"? Think about the times you may have said, "I would do_____, but...."; "I could do that, but..."; "I want to try that, but...". How are your "buts" preventing you from being all you can be?

Take Initiative

I love the famous quote, "Some people make things happen, some watch things happen, while others wonder what happened (after the fact)". Which one are you? Do you wait around for others to fix things and make things right or do you take the initiative? Do you wait for your parents to tell you to do your chores or do you do them on your own?

Initiative:

The power or ability to begin or to follow through energetically with a plan or task; the ability or attitude to start something.

I think we should all adopt the motto of Nike Shoes which simply says, "*Just Do It*". If you can begin to make taking the initiative a habit while you are still young, I am convinced it will take you places and open doors like you couldn't imagine. So often, people will sit around and complain, polluting the air with comments about what they would do and what others should do, yet, there is never any action to back it up. Don't be one of those people. Martin Luther

King Jr., summarized it best when he said, "You don't have to see the whole staircase, just take the first step".

Take Responsibility

Depending on the circumstances, taking responsibility can often be a little frightening because it creates an opportunity for you to fail miserably, and this is one of the biggest fears of people and the reason, so many people never, ever try.

Instead they will have a long list of things they "would have", "could have" and "should have" done but a very short list of actual things they did.

PRICELESS PRINCIPLE - #13

Remember, the secret to getting ahead is getting started. Write a plan for the future and work your plan.

PRICELESS POINTERS
(ON SELF-DISCIPLINE –
GOAL SETTING & ATTITUDE)

- You don't have to be great to get started, but you do have to get started to be great. - Anonymous

- Take action and responsibility for your future. If you don't, a year from now you may wish you had started today.

- You might not be able to do everything related to your goals all at once, but you can do something.

- Make specific and realistic goals and write them down.

- While you may not be able to change certain things in life (like your parents, teachers or certain situations), you do have the power to change your attitude.

Chapter 14
TREASURE BEYOND MEASURE
(SELF-CONTROL – BOYS, DATING & SEX)

There is no way I could write a book for teen girls and leave out a chapter devoted to love and relationships. Especially since girls spend a great deal of time dreaming and fantasizing about finding love and being in a relationship.

Have you ever noticed that when you go into a jewelry store that real diamonds and other expensive jewels are placed in a display case, safely protected under lock and key, while the costume jewelry sits on top of the display counter for everyone to touch and feel? Why is it that when it comes to the real deal, you must have a key to gain access? Well, that's simple; it's because of its value.

When we think about rare gems that makes perfect sense, but why do the rules change when we think of something much more precious? Much like the jewelry display case that protects diamonds and keeps people from touching, handling and stealing them, it is important for girls to create the same type of boundaries and barriers when it comes to their bodies, their hearts and their minds.

When we don't recognize our value or are fooled into thinking that our value is based on our bodies, it's just like equating ourselves to costume jewelry, instead of the real deal.

Just think about it, would you let a valuable, priceless piece of jewelry be passed around from person to person? Of course not. Yet, many of us allow ourselves to be passed around from relationship to relationship, simply because we don't know better.

The Most Precious Gift

Love, sex and romance are wonderful things, but only when operating under the purpose for which they were created, which is in a healthy, committed marriage. Did you catch that? Marriage is the proper key that should be used to unlock the display case.

Many times, girls are tricked, manipulated or persuaded into having sex or using their bodies physically to please and tease others. As a result, they fail to realize that when it comes to sex it is by far one of the most precious gifts of all, and was created to be unwrapped on their wedding day and given as the ultimate gift of love to their husband.

This is not to make you ashamed of anything that you have done or experienced, but to simply open your eyes and make you aware of your true value. Please know that egardless of your past or your current situation, when you know better you can always do better.

No matter what you may have thought in the past or what others have told you, you are worth the wait. Your value is beyond measure and is not determined by your body or by what others think. Your value and worth is determined by God. Make a decision to believe what He says about you and begin to line your words and actions up with that very thing.

Playing With Fire

David Mahan, an international speaker and founder of Frontline Communication, spoke to a group of girls at our annual Girls of Greatness Conference, and I will never forget him using an analogy of a fireplace in someone's home.

I think we can all agree that a fire is great on a cold winter night, if you are sitting around a fireplace, watching a movie, with your cozy PJ's sipping cocoa or eating popcorn. However, the same fire would not be good if it moved beyond the fireplace, catching a rug on fire, which in turn catches the sofa on fire and eventually spreading throughout the whole house, and burning it down. Now that would not be good, right?

Well the fire itself wasn't bad. In fact, we can agree that the fire in the fireplace was a good thing. But when the fire began to move beyond the boundaries it was created to remain within, then it turned ugly and dangerous, really fast; ultimately causing damage and destruction which could have led to death.

Well, the same is true when it comes to sex. The reality is that God created sex and He gave us sexual desires. Sex is not bad. In fact, it can be one of the most beautiful acts of love and intimacy when kept within the boundaries of marriage. It is when you step outside these boundaries in which it was created that it can be dangerous and have lifelong consequences.

We all know the consequence that comes to the minds of most and that is teen pregnancy, but that is just touching the surface. Sex is more than just a physical act. It affects you completely, physically, mentally, emotionally, financially and spiritually. When it comes to the consequences of sex the effect goes beyond the physical. There are multiple consequences, including:

- **Physical Consequences** – which include pregnancy, sexually transmitted diseases (many of which have no cure or could cause cancer, infertility or even cost you your life).

- **Emotional Consequences** – which range from everything from heartache, worry, regret, hopelessness, depression, sadness, lack of self-respect, guilt or shame.

Social Consequences – which include damaging your reputation; attracting the wrong people for the wrong reasons, due to a lack of trust or communication.

- **Mental Consequences** – which can include low self-esteem, lack of focus, jealousy, anger, obsession, being paranoid that others are talking about you.

- **Relational Consequences** – which can include possible changes in your relationship with your parents or family, changes in your friendships, or unhealthy dating habits, and emotional ties.

- **Spiritual Consequences** – which can include feeling disappointed, guilty, shameful or feeling separated from God.

Are any of these consequences worth it? I am going to go ahead and say, NO! As a Priceless GEM I want you to live your best life, and the best way to ensure that you reach your goals and live your best life is by making a decision that you are worth the wait and that you want to save sex until marriage.

The Real Deal on Sexually Transmitted Diseases (STD's)

While the areas noted above are equally important, I want to take a moment to focus specifically on physical consequences. When it comes to Sexually Transmitted Diseases (STD's), you're opening a door you may not be able to close. In fact, many STD's can be considered a gift that keeps on giving. Every year more than 15 million cases of STD's are reported in the U.S. with a large number of new cases being among teenagers.

Teens are especially susceptible to STD's due to their anatomy and because they have a lower level of antibodies (which fight infection) than adults.

While STD's don't discriminate and both girls and guys are also at risk of contracting STD's, unfortunately girls suffer the most. According to a survey conducted by the CDC in 2008, it was estimated that one in four (26 percent) young women between the ages of 14 and 19 in the United States – or 3.2 million teenage girls – were infected with at least one of the most common sexually transmitted diseases (human papillomavirus (HPV), Chlamydia, herpes simplex virus, and trichomoniasis).

These numbers are high among teen girls specifically because of the nature of their reproductive organs. Many STD's survive best where it is dark, moist, and warm. Because the female's reproductive system is mostly interior, her body is more easily infected. Compared to a male, she also has a larger surface area of tissue that certain STD's might affect. Furthermore, a female's body is exposed to infectious diseases for a longer period of time after intercourse. These biological differences make females more likely to catch certain STD's.

he risk of infection is greater for young girls and teens because their cervix is immature and more sensitive and vulnerable to infections. In most cases, when a young woman reaches her mid-twenties, the cervix will have matured.

In addition, many girls and women are often asymptomatic, which means they may have an STD without knowing because they have delayed symptoms. When there are no symptoms, the disease(s) can still be transferred, and long-term damage can be caused including infertility (not being able to have a baby), pelvic inflammatory disease (PID), or an ectopic pregnancy.

This chart shows on the left the number of sexual partners, and on the right the number of people potentially exposed (assuming that everyone has the same sexual partners). It demonstrates the real risks of having casual sex and how your risks multiply with each encounter. It's not a game worth playing. Even if you are in a committed relationship with your boyfriend, you must factor in any previous partners that either of you had in the past.

# Sexual Partners	Sexual Exposure Chart (if every person has only had the same partners as you)	Number of People Exposed to
1		1
2		3
3		7
4		15
5		31
6		63
7		127
8		255
9		511
10		1023

Myth Busters

There is a lot of information out in the world through the internet, friends, magazines and television, but as a Priceless GEM it is important to me that you be equipped with the facts.

Myth #1 – Everyone is doing it.

Actually, everyone is NOT doing it. According to a survey conducted in 2009 by the CDC, 54% of high school students are NOT having sex.

Myth #2 – I can practice "Safe Sex".

There is no such thing as "Safe Sex". We have been conditioned to think that condoms provide protection and keep people safe, but unfortunately not safe enough.

Condoms can reduce risks but no condom can totally eliminate them. According to the Medical Institute, if used 100% of the time (which is uncommon), a condom only reduces the risk of certain STD's, like gonorrhea and Chlamydia, about 50% of the time.

And it has been proven that even with a condom, there are several STD's that can still be transmitted through skin-to-skin contact (like HPV and Herpes).

Even more important is the fact that a condom can't protect your heart, nor can it protect you from the list of other consequences noted earlier.

Myth #3 – No one I know has an STD.

While I can't tell you who, I can guarantee you that you know someone who does have an STD.

You can't tell by looking at them. In fact many people who have STD's have no clue because they are what is called asymptomatic, which basically means they have no signs or symptoms. So in other words, they could actually be carrying a virus and passing it on to others without even knowing.

Myth #4 – If I have already had sex, it's too late to practice abstinence.

This is one of the biggest lies I think most people fall for. If a person has had sex before, they CAN make a decision to stop and commit to living a life of abstinence. In my opinion, it is one of the bravest and wisest decisions a person can make.

Myth #5 – If I have sex it will show my boyfriend how much I love him and we will stay together.

That sounds so beautiful on paper and in the movies, but in reality, very rarely do young couples remain together and go on to marry and live happily ever after. Think about it; do you think you have already met your future husband? Chances are your answer is NO WAY!!!

Many teen girls start having sex for reasons other than desire. They have sex because they want attention, affection, acceptance, and a host of other reasons. They are often searching for love in all the wrong places, and mistakenly use sex when what they are actually seeking is love. Lots of teenage girls give their most prized possession (themselves) away to "keep" a guy, only to find out he will leave anyway.

Soul Tie

While many people may think sex is just a physical act, that is not the case. Sex was created by God and was intended for marriage, designed for pleasure, but also for bonding and creating oneness. Even though our society has tried to change the rules when it comes to sex, the purpose and the effects remain the same.

Every time two people have sex, not only are they coming together physically, but they are coming together mentally and spiritually, creating a Soul Tie. So, long after that relationship has ended and the two have moved on, there is still a connection that has been made and that will forever remain. This is why casual sex, hooking up and friends-with-benefits doesn't work. Don't be fooled into making choices that can affect you the rest of your life.

Stolen Treasure

When it comes to sex and your virginity, it is something that should be given, not taken. Unfortunately, in many cases, young girls and women have situations where someone may violate them emotionally, verbally or sexually through rape, incest or molestation. According to most reliable studies of child sexual abuse in the United States, as many as one in three girls and one in seven boys will be sexually abused at some point in their childhood.

Over 70% of girls under the age of 18 who have had sex either didn't want it to happen or had mixed feelings about the encounter. If you or someone you know has experienced abuse of any kind, let me begin by telling you how truly sorry I am that you ever had to endure something so cruel, horrible and violent. No matter what the circumstances, you didn't deserve it. It wasn't your fault.

If you have been dealing alone with the scars from your past, I encourage you to get help. If you can't talk to your parents, tell a trusted adult, school counselor or friend. There are resources and support groups that can help walk you through the steps of healing.

Despite what you have faced, I want you to know that you are a treasure beyond measure and your value is untouched. You are not only precious, but you are strong and you are resilient.

To Date, or To Wait

Knowing who you are, understanding your value and making a decision to be abstinent, doesn't mean that life ends and you can never have fun and live a "normal" life. Being abstinent, doesn't mean that you can't have guy friends, hang-out or even date. In fact, it means just the opposite. It just means that you have to create boundaries and make decisions with your future in mind.

When it comes to making a decision to date or to wait, I would suggest you begin to ask yourself a series of questions and discuss your thoughts with your parents:

- *What is my purpose for dating? Is it to find my husband? Is it to interact with guys? Is it to learn more about what I like and what I don't?*

- *What qualities are important in a relationship? What are the qualities and character traits of my future husband?*

- *Why do I want to date? Is it because my friends are pressuring me? Because I am curious? Because I don't want to seem weird? Because I don't want to loose him?*

- *Why do we want/need to be exclusive? How would this help or hurt?*

- *Where can this relationship go? What do I want to get out of this relationship? How is it most likely to end (in marriage or in break-up)?*

- *Is there a way that we can spend time together and build our friendship without dating?*

- *Will he respect my commitment and decision to be abstinent? Will he support or distract me?*

Creating Boundaries

When it comes to dating, boys and relationships, it is important to create boundaries that no one can cross. These boundaries need to be set by you ahead of time, and communicated clearly. It seems pretty simple, but you would be surprised how many people allow others to set their boundaries for them or they let the situation determine their boundaries.

Just as a jewelry display case provides protection and keeps real jewels safe from theft, dust and debris, the boundaries we set can protect us. Without boundaries, it is easy for others to use you and take advantage of you physically, emotionally and even financially.

Why Waiting Works

- **It's Effective** - Abstinence is the only 100% way to avoid the physical, emotional, mental, financial and spiritual consequences.

- **It Can Increase Your Self-Esteem & Self-Respect** - Waiting will increase your self-respect, will help you gain the respect of others and will teach you to respect others.

- **It Will Help You Avoid Mr. Wrong** - Waiting will help you find the right mate (someone who values you for the person you are). You will spend more time getting to know each other.

- **It Can Help You Avoid Drama** - Waiting means a clear conscience (no guilt) and peace of mind (no conflicts, worrying or regret).

- **It Can Help You Build Character** - By practicing the virtues involved in waiting; such as faithfulness, self-control, modesty, good judgment, courage, and genuine respect for self and others; you are developing the kind of character that will make you a good marriage partner and help you attract the kind of person you would like to marry.

- **It Can Help Make Your Marriage Stronger** - Waiting can mean a better sexual relationship in marriage (free of comparisons with other premarital partners, free of sexual flashbacks and a relationship based on trust). By waiting, you are being faithful to your spouse even before you meet him.

You Set The Standard

As a Priceless GEM, always remember that you set the standard and when you do, those who are worthy will follow. Remember you are a Treasure Beyond Measure and despite the pressures you may feel daily, you are special and well worth the wait.

PRICELESS PRINCIPLE - #14
Remember, you are a Treasure Beyond Measure and your body is a precious gift, created by God.

PRICELESS POINTERS
(ON SELF-CONTROL - BOYS, DATING & SEX)

- Consider group dating. This allows you to observe guys in a pressure-free environment and to see how they interact with others.

- Remember you don't owe anyone an explanation.

- Talk to your parents and never do things behind their backs.

- Avoid places, situations and conversations that will lead to temptation or lead you to compromise your commitment to yourself.

- Focus on your future. When abstinence gets difficult, remember your future goals and the reasons you have chosen to start over.

Chapter 15
PAID IN FULL
(SALVATION)

When it comes to the price of real diamonds the price can vary from several hundred dollars to millions of dollars. I think we would agree that what most diamonds symbolize is something of value.

When my husband made the decision to ask me for my hand in marriage, it was a pretty important decision. And as you can imagine, part of him sealing the deal was his willingness and desire to purchase and place a wedding ring on my finger. He was careful in the selection of the "perfect" ring to fit me, my lifestyle and my personality. He wanted to make sure that every time I looked at it that it would remind me of his love and be a symbol of our commitment to one another.

Although he worked hard and saved his hard-earned money for my beautiful wedding ring, the value far exceeds the actual cost. When you actually think about it, what price can you place on true love? I think the price of love is immeasurable, which means it is actually beyond measure.

A Love Like No Other

Most girls dream of one day finding a love like no other. Meeting their prince charming, whether on a white horse or in a white sports car, I am not mad at a sister for dreaming. I think it's a great thing to dream about your future and to desire to be in love and to be loved. I pray you will wait, save yourself and make a lifetime commitment to the one person who is deserving of your hand. As I tell girls of all ages, you are worth the wait. Don't allow the pressures of this world to cause you to sell yourself short or to settle for less than God's very best. Why settle for less when God wants so much more for you?

Your value was actually determined before you were ever born. God's Word says, "Before I formed you in the womb I knew you, before you were born I set you apart"; Jeremiah 1:5. You are part of God's perfect plan, and guess what? He doesn't make mistakes.

The very One who hung the moon and the stars in the sky, is the same one who handcrafted you in all your uniqueness and blessed the world with your presence.

Every beautiful diamond was handcrafted by a Gem Maker who from the very beginning was able to recognize the potential of a precious stone. With patience, diamonds are loved, just like you are loved and I'm not talking about the superficial love from people who are looking for something in return.

You are loved by the One who created you. He deposited greatness inside of you, before the beginning of time. God created everything about you, every fine detail from the color of your eyes, to your body frame, whether it is full of curves or straight as a board. None of that matters to Him.

Some tend to think, that because of their history or stories that have been passed down, that perhaps they were a mistake. But in reality, none of us are a mistake. Regardless of how our parents hooked up, whether they are still together or even in our lives, the fact remains that each one of us was created by God and formed in His image and likeness which makes us pretty incredible.

Our introduction into the world on that marvelous day we were born didn't take Him by surprise. In fact, I'm pretty sure the angels in heaven rejoiced and celebrated because they knew that we were being sent into the world for a specific purpose and to do great things.

You may be one of those people who secretly thinks, "There is no way that God could love me. I'm not smart enough, spiritual enough, I'm not good enough." Well you couldn't be more wrong. God loves you just the way you are, mistakes, flaws, quirks and all. There is nothing that you have done or that you can ever do that is too deep for Him to handle or to forgive.

This is difficult for some people to realize, because they are used to people who give love and affection based on conditions. The love of people doesn't begin to compare with God's love for us. He created you in your mother's womb and He knows everything about you right down to the number of hairs on your head (Luke 12:7).

The Ultimate Price

When you think of everything that you have been reminded of in this book, from you being precious, strong, set apart and created for a purpose; let this point be the one that you remember most of all: Your value is beyond measure and the ultimate price has already been paid for you and for the incredible future that's awaiting.

If you are wondering what in the world I mean by that, it's really simple. God created you and with it He created a plan and purpose for your life. He knew when and where you would be born, the obstacles and challenges you would face in this crazy world, and He never loses track of how precious and valuable you are to Him. Not in dollars or cents, but through the sacrifice of His son Jesus Christ.

Whether you already know this or may be hearing this for the very first time, it all boils down to this. God loved you so much that He allowed His very son to be sacrificed for your sake and mine. God knew that we would never be perfect and that we would always fall short in one way or another, but that didn't stop His love for us or His plan for our lives. He knew we would struggle, and that sometimes we would fall, but even that didn't stop Him from loving us and setting us apart for such a time as this.

He created us, He loves us and He allowed His only son, the only perfect person to ever live, to die a cruel and brutal death on a wooden cross in a place called Calvary so that you and I could live. And it was not so that we would simply live, but that we would live an abundant, joy-filled and purposeful life.

Now when you think about God's ultimate love and the ultimate price He paid, I know there is no other who can compare. When I think about how easily we allow ourselves to get distracted, discouraged and derailed, it is as if we are pawning the ring that Jesus purchased with His life.

His blood was sacrificed for our burdens, our pain, our frustrations, our confusion, our depression, our weaknesses,

How Priceless is your unfailing love!

Psalm 36:7

our illnesses, and for ALL our shortcomings. It's that simple. He traded the long list of things that were wrong with us, things that were created to destroy us, to steal our joy and to keep us from His best. He paid the ultimate price with His life, so we could have life and live it to the fullest.

So with that, you may be wondering, how do you begin to live your life to the fullest? How can you actually begin to believe the things written in this book and live them out on a daily basis? Well it begins by simply acknowledging with your mouth and with your heart that God loves you and that He paid the ultimate price through His son, Jesus Christ, who died for your sin and shortcomings. And the last thing is to simply invite God, who I call the ultimate GEM Maker, into your heart.

He loves you and He wants to walk this thing out with you. He wants you to lean on Him and trust in Him. He wants to take you places and help you do things that you would never imagine.

Forget What You Know

Knowing about someone and knowing them personally are too different things. For instance, I know about a lot of famous people. I can tell you the movies they have appeared in or their Top 10 songs. I can read about them in the latest magazines and may even be able to tell you about their interests or their families. But that doesn't mean that I know them. It's not until I have met them and developed a relationship over time, that I really come to know them on a personal level.

When it comes to God, the same is true. Most people know about God but few people really know Him personally. They may have heard about Him when they were little or, believe it or not, they may even go to church and sing about Him every week, but yet not know Him.

There is nothing greater on earth than knowing Him personally for yourself. It may sound bizarre, but I am telling you the truth. I can share this with confidence because I have experienced His ultimate love in my life and it is beyond any words that I can describe. Inviting God into my heart was the most important decision I have made in my entire life.

Growing up, I believed God was real, but my view of Him was all wrong. I was clearly afraid of God and I envisioned Him as a hard, rigid God who was always ready to cast judgment on imperfect people. Boy was I ever wrong!

After I invited Him into my heart and got to know Him for myself, I began to learn that my view of God was totally the opposite. I learned that while God is strong and mighty (I mean think about it, He created the universe), He is also loving, caring, compassionate and kind. Not only that, I learned that He loves little me just the way I am.

I have to always remember that everyone's view of God is different and can be based on all kinds of things, so I like to say unless you have a real relationship with God, forget what you think you know.

So often we have been exposed to a counterfeit, copy-cat God which has either turned us off, disappointed us or left us unmoved, unimpressed, and unchanged. For others we may be familiar with church and with religion, but have no clue about a relationship with God.

I want you to think about the word "relationship". When you think of that word, what comes to mind? For me I think of some of my closest friends. I think of someone I can talk to; someone who loves me unconditionally; someone I enjoy spending time with and who is always there for me; someone I can be real with; someone who wants the best for me. Well God wants to be all that and more in our lives.

We have an opportunity to be introduced to the true and living God who loves us, cares for us and has a plan for our lives. This thing is not about religion and rituals, nor is it about being perfect and having it all together. In fact it's about just the opposite. It is about acknowledging that we fall short and that even when we don't have it all together we can ask Him to come into our lives and help us make sense of things.

Perfect People Need Not Apply

I was always under the impression that God was looking for "perfect people", and I knew I was far from perfect. But what I learned instead is that there are no "perfect people". We all fall short in one area or another, but the good thing is that it doesn't matter when it comes to God. He loves us just the way we are and He has everything we need. If we are in need of joy, we can find joy in Him. If we are lonely, we can find a friend like no other in Him. If we are sick we can find the ultimate physician in Him. If we are confused, we can find wisdom on what to do in Him. There is nothing on earth that we stand in need of that He can't provide.

Designer Original

Part of living the ultimate life God created for you is by entering into a personal relationship with Him. I mean, really getting to know Him, because He already knows you.

The one thing I can say about God is that He is a gentleman, and He will not force Himself on anyone. What He wants more than anything is for us to welcome Him into our hearts so He can reveal His plan and purpose for our lives. He wants to gently mold and shape each of us into the Priceless GEMS we were created to be. And at the right time He wants to reveal His masterpiece, a true designer original, by placing us on display in all our brilliance for the entire world to see.

The God Shaped Hole

Before I knew any of this I had an emotional hole in my heart. I tried filling that hole with so many things. I tried filling it with friendships and being accepted. I tried filling it with boys and relationships. I tried filling it with money and stuff. No matter what I tried, it never worked. It wasn't until one of my high school friends introduced me to God that my life began to change and that hole began to be filled slowly but surely.

Now I will be honest, it took a little time for things to come together. As I said in the beginning, I was a piece of work. But as I learned more about God and about His love for me, my mind and thoughts began to change and started to line up with His thoughts of me. Before long, my words began to change, and things became clearer and clearer.

Now, if you don't currently have a relationship with God, you too have an opportunity to have your life totally transformed for the best. It's not hard nor is it complicated. It doesn't require you to stand in a church or to set an appointment with a pastor or priest. It's as simple as opening your heart and your mouth and inviting God in, wherever you are.

It doesn't matter what you've done or where you've been. But there's more... not only does a relationship with God impact you in this present life but it also has an eternal effect. That simply means that when you die and take your final breath on earth, you can also be assured that you will go to Heaven.

A Friend Like No Other

I can't begin to tell you how much that one decision has affected my life and totally turned it completely around for the better. It was truly the best decision I could have ever made.

One of the most incredible things that I learned after I invited God into my heart and began to develop a relationship with Him, was that He is a friend like no other. Not only is He patient and never ever too busy for me, but He loves me unconditionally. He gives me wisdom, strength, joy, peace and comfort. I can laugh with Him and cry with Him. I can tell Him my deepest secrets and keep it real with Him, without fear of shame, guilt or rejection.

He helped me begin to see myself as He sees me. He accepted me for who I was (mistakes, issues and all). And through His love letters and promises to me (and you) which are sprinkled throughout His Word (the Bible), I began to heal, forgive, and find joy and purpose for my life.

I plugged into a wonderful church where I was able to learn more about Him and grow in my faith. I can honestly say, I am still learning to this very day, and experiencing a love like no other.

The Basic ABC's of Salvation

A Priceless GEM named Shelby recently broke down the simplicity of Salvation better than I have ever heard. Accepting the ultimate gift of salvation is as simple as remembering ABC.

 Acknowledge - that you don't have it all together and are not perfect (also referred to as sin).

Believe - in your heart that Jesus paid the ultimate price by dying on a cross for your short comings (sins).

Confess - with your mouth that 'Jesus is Lord' and that He died for you, and make a commitment to follow Him (by praying, reading the Bible and getting plugged into a strong church where you can learn God's Word and grow in your faith).

That's all there is to it. It's not complicated at all, just a simple acknowledgement, belief and confession. It's not about an eloquent confession with fancy words or an extravagant ceremony. It's about simply opening your mouth and inviting God into your heart.

If you have never invited Him in but you desire to do so, simply say the words below:

God, I thank you for paying the ultimate price for me and sending Jesus to die for my sins. I know I am not perfect and there are areas in my life where I fall short. I am sorry for anything I may have said or done over the years that weren't right or were outside of your perfect plan for my life. I thank you for loving and accepting me just the way I am and thank you for the awesome and mighty plan you have for my future. I invite you into my heart and into my life and I want you to help me be all you created me to be. – Amen

The decision to accept Jesus is a personal choice. As I said earlier, He is a gentleman and He doesn't want to come anywhere He is not welcomed. It is my heartfelt desire that you will invite Him into your heart, and experience His love firsthand.

If you already have a personal relationship with God or have just accepted Him into your heart today by reading the previous prayer, CONGRUATIONS!!! If you are unsure or have decided you're not interested, please know that God's door is always open and you have a direct connection 24/7.

Shine

In closing I challenge you to take the things that you have read in this book and apply them to your life, starting today. Make a decision to allow your brilliance to shine for the entire world to see.

As this portion of you personal journey of self-discover comes to a close, I want to leave you with a small gift. The poem on the next page was written with you in mind. In a moment, I want you to read it aloud with confidence and boldness. If you need to, fold the page down, commit it to memory, take a picture of it and save it on your phone or whatever you need to do to re-visit it often.

As you enter the next phase of your journey, I hope you do so with new confidence and a clear understanding of Who and Whose you are. I hope you will begin to love the skin you're in embrace your unique gifts and talents. I hope that you will no longer place your worth and value in what others think of you, but remember the only opinion that matters is yours and Gods.

Continue to invest in yourself, pick your words carefully, surround yourself with positive people and press forward. Remember, the difference between a carbon rock and a priceless gem, is the priceless gem withstood the pressure, the process and the polishing and came out more beautiful, bold and brilliant as a result.

A PRICELESS GEM

I am a Priceless Gem, unique in design.
With value and potential, I was created to shine.

Created with gifts, talents and abilities that are rare.
I celebrate my uniqueness, and I have no need to
compare.

My hair, my lips, and my hips I've learned to embrace;
And every fine detail of my beautiful face.

From head to toe, I am a Priceless treasure;
with beauty, boldness and brilliance beyond measure.

I am smart, created for a purpose, and my future is bright;
I am committed to making a difference in this world,
and to being a light.

I understand with clarity that I am a Priceless Gem;
And everything I need, God has already provided within.

I now embrace who I am, because I know without a doubt;
I wasn't created to fit in, I was designed to stand out!!!

- By Nicole Steele

PRICELESS PRINCIPLE - #15

Remember, we are truly Priceless GEMS. God paid the ultimate price for you and me through His Son Jesus Christ.
No value can ever compare.

PRICELESS POINTERS
(ON SALVATION)

- ❖ God is not interested in religion; He is interested in a personal relationship with you.

- ❖ Remember, God's love is unconditional, and can't be earned by our work or deeds.

- ❖ God won't come where He is not invited. Salvation is a choice.

- ❖ You are a designer original and NOT a copy, so boldly walk in the knowledge that you are precious and set apart.

- ❖ God will never leave you nor forsake you.

PRICELESS PROMISES

BEAUTY
"Your beauty should not come from outward adornment, such as elaborate hairstyles and the wearing of gold jewelry or fine clothes. Rather, it should be that of your inner self, the unfading beauty of a gentle and quiet spirit, which is of great worth in God's sight." – **1 Peter 3:3-4 (NIV)**

BLESSINGS
"The Lord will make you the head, not the tail. If you pay attention to the commands of the Lord your God that I give you this day and carefully follow them, you will always be at the top, never at the bottom." – **Deuteronomy 28:13 (NIV)**

COURAGE
"God is our refuge and strength, an ever-present help in trouble." – **Psalm 46:1 (NIV)**

FEAR
"For God has not given us a spirit of fear and timidity, but of power, love, and self-discipline." – **2 Timothy 1:7 (NLT)**

GIVING
Give, and it will be given to you. A good measure, pressed down, shaken together and running over, will be poured into your lap. For with the measure you use, it will be measured to you." – **Luke 6:38 (NIV)**

HOPE
"For I know the plans I have for you declares the Lord, plans to prosper you and not to harm you, plans to give you hope and a future." – **Jeremiah 29:11 (NIV)**

NEEDS
"And God is able to bless you abundantly, so that in all things at all times, having all that you need, you will abound in every good work." – **Corinthians 9:8 (NIV)**

PARENTS	*"Honor your father and your mother, so that you may live long in the land the LORD your God is giving you."* – **Exodus 20:12 (NIV)**
PROTECTION	*"But no weapon that is formed against you shall prosper, and every tongue that shall rise against you in judgment you shall show to be in the wrong."* – **Isaiah 54:17 (AMP)**
SELF IMAGE	You were created in God's Image - *"So God created man in his own image, in the image of God he created them; male and female he created them."* – **Genesis 1:27 (NIV)**
STRENGTH	*"I can do everything through Him who gives me strength."* – **Philippians 4:13 (NIV)**
STRESS	*"Give all your worries and cares to God, for he cares about you."* – **1 Peter 5:7 (NLT)**
SUCCESS	*"We are more than conquerors through him who loved us."* – **Romans 8:37 (NIV)**
TRUST	*"I will never desert you, nor will I ever forsake you."* – **Hebrews 13:5 (NAS)**
WISDOM	*"Listen to advice and accept instruction, and in the end you will be wise."* – **Proverbs 19:20 (NIV)**
	"If any of you lack wisdom, he should ask God who gives generously to all without finding fault, and it will be given to him." – **James 1:5 (NIV)**
	"Call to me and I will answer you and tell you great and unsearchable things you do not know." – **Jeremiah 33:3 (NIV)**

SOURCES

All Made Up – A girls guide to seeing through celebrity hype ... and celebrating real beauty, Audrey Brashich

Aspire – Live Your Life to Be Free, Scott Phelps

Center for Disease Control – www.cdc.gov

Checklist for Life for Teens, Thomas Nelson

Re-Arranging Your Mental Furniture, Ken Gaub

The Curse of Comparison, Jimmy Evans of Marriage Today

The Girl's Life – Guide to Growing Up, Karen Bokram and Alexis Sinex

The Medical Institute – www.medinstitute.org

The Naked Truth About Sex, Love and Relationships, Lakita Garth

The Power of Abstinence, Kristine Napier

The Real Majority – www.therealmajority.com

The Success Principles for Teens, Jack Canfield & Kent Healy

True Images NIV Bible

U.S. Department of Health & Human Services, www.hhs.gov

What Guys See That Girls Don't...or Do They, Sharon Daugherty

www.Chasity.com

Learn more about the companion products:

Priceless E-book

Priceless Workbook

Priceless - Prayer Journal

Priceless - Small Group Leaders Guide

Priceless - Bible Study Leaders Guide

Priceless - Bible Study Participant Guide

Priceless - Bible Study Set
(Includes bible study leaders guide and 10 participant guides)

Priceless - Parents Pack
(Includes paperback book, workbook and parent guide)

Priceless - Party Pack
(Includes everything needed to host a Priceless Party)

Also inquire about interest in coordinating special guest appearances, speaking opportunities or small group workshops by Nicole Steele and the Priceless Team.

GemMakers
Publishing

To provide feedback or obtain more information on
A Priceless GEM or other publications, programs and
projects of author, Nicole Steele

Call: (404) 477-GEMS *(4367)*
Visit: www.APricelessGem.com
Email: info@APricelessGem.com
Facebook: APricelessGem
Twitter: APricelessGem

For more information on
Diamond In The Rough Youth Development Program, Inc.

Call: (678) 376-9676
Visit: www.ditr.org
Email: info@ditr.org
Facebook: DiamondInTheRoughInc
Twitter: DITR_Inc